The Role of the Scroll

ALSO BY THOMAS FORREST KELLY

Capturing Music: The Story of Notation

Music Then and Now

Quicunqꝫ legerit coram co co coram hac septem orationes
cum totidem pater nr̄ et aue maria merebitur qua
draginta octo milia annorum. et quadraginta ann
uos. et quadraginta octo dies indulgentiarum

dñe ihū xp̄e adoro te
in cruce pendentem. et
coronā spineā in capi
te portantem. deprecor
te. ut crux tua liberet
me ab angelo percuti
ente. Pr̄ nr̄. Aue maria.

O dñe ihū xp̄e ado
ro te in cruce uul
neratū. felle et aceto
potatū. deprecor te. ut tua vulnera sint reme
dium anime mee. Pater noster. Aue maria.

O dñe ihū xp̄e adoro te in sepulchro positū
mirra et aromatibꝫ conditū. deprecor te
ut tua mors sit vita mea. Pater nr̄. Aue maria.

O dñe ihū xp̄e adoro te descendentē ad infe
ros. liberantemcꝫ captiuos. deprecor te.
ne pmittas me illuc introire. Pr̄ nr̄. Aue maria

O dñe ihū xp̄e adoro te resurgentē a mortu
is. ascendentem in cælis. sedentemcꝫ ad dē
dexterā patris. deprecor te. miserere mei. nr̄. Aue.

O dñe ihū xp̄e pastor bone. iustos cõserua
peccatores iustifica. omnibꝫ fidelibꝫ mi
serere. et ppicius esto michi peccatori. Pr̄ nr̄. Aue mā

O dñe ihū xp̄e fili dei viui. rogo te per illā
amaritudinē quā sustinuisti in cruce max
ime in illa hora quando aīa tua sāctissima de tuo
benedicto corpe egressa est. miserere aīe mee in egres
su suo. Pr̄ nr̄. Aue. Collecta ex deuotione addit

O dñe ihū xp̄e fili dei viui. qui sāctissime passiōis
tue misteriū br̄o gregorio famulo tuo mi
rabiliter reuelasti. da michi misero peccatori illam
pfecte consequi remissionē peccatorū et indulgentiā
quā idem venerabilis antistes tuus et alij sūmi
pontifices de plenitudine potestatis aplice oībus

The Role of
the Scroll

An Illustrated Introduction to
Scrolls in the Middle Ages

Thomas Forrest Kelly

W. W. NORTON & COMPANY
INDEPENDENT PUBLISHERS SINCE 1923
NEW YORK • LONDON

For information about permission to reproduce selections from this book, write to
Permissions, W. W. Norton & Company, Inc., 500 Fifth Avenue, New York, NY 10110

For information about special discounts for bulk purchases, please contact W. W. Norton
Special Sales at specialsales@wwnorton.com or 800-233-4830

Manufacturing by Versa Press
Book design by Dana Sloan
Production manager: Anna Oler

ISBN 978-0-393-28503-1

W. W. Norton & Company, Inc., 500 Fifth Avenue, New York, N.Y. 10110
www.wwnorton.com

W. W. Norton & Company Ltd., 15 Carlisle Street, London W1D 3BS

1 2 3 4 5 6 7 8 9 0

TO WILLIAM STONEMAN

Contents

(*Opposite*) Detail from *The Guthlac Roll* (British Library, Harley Rolls Y6, f. 18r), the last of 18 roundels. (*See pages 132–133.*)

Preface

Scrolls are fascinating objects that have always been shrouded by an intriguing kind of aura, and a quality of somehow standing outside of time. Scrolls from the Middle Ages are particularly interesting to me, as I have come to encounter them again and again as I conduct research on this period in time. They can appear as everything from ancient diplomas to modern computer screens, and although we are used to long pieces of paper rolled up—newsprint, paper towels—a scroll as a vehicle for writing is an unusual object in our world. We are more used to books and magazines—all codices, as the Romans would have said—with their folded and nested sheets written on both sides.

As individual objects, ancient and medieval scrolls hold our attention by their age, often by their beauty, and by the fact that their format is unusual. You'll find many of the most beautiful and unusual scrolls illustrated in this very book.

But more than a compilation of beautiful scrolls, this book is about the scroll as a phenomenon. I ask questions such as: Why did people make scrolls? Why did they make scrolls in the Middle Ages after the codex had become the standard way to record a long text? There are several reasons for this, I think, and they are good ones. The chapters that follow are centered on those reasons—from needing to represent space and time on a long line to providing a way of adding to a list and being able to roll something so tightly that it fits into a private amulet.

My fascination with scrolls brings me back to a day spent at the Vatican Library. While I was doing research for a book on the illustrated *Exultet* scrolls of southern Italy (they will come up here, too) and having a coffee break (the 11 a.m. coffee break at the Vatican Library's bar is an international rendezvous, a hub of scholarly exchange), I told a friend what I was working on. "That's interesting," she said, "How many medieval scrolls are there?"

Having no idea of the answer, I went back to the library and started looking at books about the history of the book, books about writing, and the like. All the experts mention that the scroll gives way to the book in the fourth century. They all refer to the beautiful south-Italian *Exultet* scrolls—but they do not say much more. The assumption seems to be that once the book, or codex, arrives, the scroll is definitively left behind.

And that's true, but not quite. There are, in fact, hundreds, probably thousands, of scrolls from the Middle Ages. (And there are still scrolls being made today, but just not very many.) Discovering this, I tried to find out as much about scrolls as I could. Eventually, the first chapter of my book on the *Exultet* scrolls was a general introduction to medieval scrolls. This present volume, however, is a broader and more comprehensive version of that first attempt.

It became a bit of a project for me to make a list of scrolls. Every time I saw one, or saw a reference to one, I put it in a file. Over a period of almost twenty years, the folder has grown quite fat. In 2014, feeling that it was time to make this study more comprehensive and systematic, I taught an interdisciplinary seminar on scrolls at Harvard, along with my colleagues Beverly Kienzle and William Stoneman. We had a wonderful group of talented graduate students in various fields: history, theology, art history, and music. I gave them my list of scrolls, and my long list of literature on scrolls, and they engaged in a treasure hunt to try and find yet more scrolls and complete the bibliography.

At the same time, we presented in the Houghton Library an exhibition of a dozen medieval scrolls belonging to Harvard University, and prepared a series of videos on medieval scrolls for HarvardX, the online learning unit of Harvard University, as part of a larger series on the history of the book. A substantial website, medievalscrolls.com, now links all this material—exhibition, database, bibliography, videos—and documents some six hundred scrolls from the Western Middle Ages. It does not, however, include scrolls in Greek: there is an ancillary list of several hundred Greek rolls, but they're not in the main list partly because the list is of Latin and western European languages, and partly because we're not convinced that the Greek list is comprehensive. But it's there, in its incomplete form.

The material on this website is the most comprehensive information on scrolls in the medieval West available in the world today. With all this resource material available worldwide, it now seems possible, and I hope desirable, to present this book to those who may be interested in the phenomenon of the scroll. This book does not seek to show everything, nor is it meant to be comprehensive and cover all past scholarship on scrolls, even though it is based on long and thorough study. (That material is on the website.) What I propose here is an exploration, a set of highlights of some of the most interesting scrolls in medieval history, and I put them in the context of the people who made them, commissioned them, and used them.

So to my friend's question—how many scrolls are there?—I have made an attempt at an answer. (About six hundred, if you limit the list to Latin and European vernacular languages, and omit the innumerable record-keeping scrolls.) But there's a second and equally important question: why make a scroll when you could make a book? This book is an attempt to answer that question.

The Role of the Scroll

CHAPTER I

Introduction to Scrolls

Why make a scroll if you have the technology to make a book? This is an introduction to the amazing, colorful, remarkable scrolls made in the Middle Ages. They range from showy documents for empresses to tiny amulets for pregnant women, and from scrolls that show their images one by one as they are unrolled to portable poetry.

Scrolls were the standard form of book in Western antiquity, and in many other cultures throughout the world. But from the fourth century onward, the codex began to supersede the scroll, and very soon it was essentially the only way that long texts were recorded.

And yet, for various reasons, people in the Middle Ages continued to make scrolls. They did not make them very often, but they did make them, and some of them are supremely beautiful. Why did people continue to make scrolls? Were they obstinate archconservatives? Or did they just not get word of the new codex technology?

My focus in this book is on the Middle Ages. From the end of the Roman Empire until the Renaissance begins (starting with the fifteenth century in Italy, let's say, depending on which scholars you heed) is a very long time, but the Middle Ages is not exactly the middle of anything. It was a period of high creativity—in phi-

FIG. 1.8B

(*Opposite*) Detail from Figure 1.8b, an Ethiopian magic scroll (*see page 19*).

losophy, science, and art—that laid the foundations for our modern civilization. It was full of talented, intelligent, and sophisticated people.

Here I focus on the scrolls of western Europe, that area that used Latin and its related languages, encompassing roughly the ancient Roman Empire. We will take a look at scrolls in other places and other cultures, but I do not attempt to discuss all scrolls from all times and places. Among the ancient Greeks and Romans, in ancient Egypt, and in many Asian cultures to discuss scrolls would be tantamount to discussing books in general. My particular interest here, and I hope yours, is in asking why people continued to make scrolls when everybody else was using codices. Each of the sections that follows is about people who made scrolls, and the fascinating objects that arise when you want to roll something up as opposed to folding along a spine.

It might be argued that the age of the codex is now over. It has had a good run, of course—from the fourth to the twenty-first century—and it will surely continue to hang on for some time to come, even though it seems its heyday has come and gone. We are now in the new age of the scroll. All you have to do is look at your computer screen, tablet, or e-reader, and just scroll down.

So then what are some of the reasons for making a scroll? As you'll see, sometimes the reason is purely practical. Scroll format is useful when you don't know at the beginning how long the text will be. A list of things can grow. You might add recipes to your cookbook, you might add people to your list, and as your list grew, so would the document that contained them. Medieval alchemical recipes, cookbooks, and other lists were probably made as scrolls so that they could be lengthened as new materials arrived.

Using length to represent time or space is another favorite reason to make a scroll. A long line might represent the road from your location to Rome, or the time elapsed between Adam and King Henry VI of England. In both cases, the scroll form allows for the use of a continuous line, not interrupted by page breaks.

Some scrolls are intensely personal and private, perhaps having been hung from a cord around the neck, or used as charms or as prompts for prayer. A little scroll with something important on it is a frequent phenomenon in the Middle Ages. Performers—singers, poets, actors—tended to use personal scrolls; this is because they are small and portable, and easily held—or concealed—in the hand. (The actor's "rôle" is originally the French word for scroll.)

In almost the opposite case, events that are specifically solemn and public may also call for scrolls. When something is important, we like to mark it with signs of antiquity and tradition. At concerts, we dress up to go and hear an orchestra whose male members often still wear white tie and tails—archaic nineteenth-century clothing. The vestments used in many churches are versions of medieval street wear. What is ancient has importance, especially today. And similarly we sometimes use the scroll form to give authenticity and solemnity to the text it bears. That's why diplomas and citations are often written on scrolls. (In the film of *The Wizard of Oz*, the death certificate for the Wicked Witch of the East is presented by the Munchkins' coroner on a scroll; it's also the form of the Scarecrow's diploma.)

For each type of scroll there are wonderful surviving examples, made by people who had a specific reason for making a scroll rather than a book. They are not so many in number, though; in the great torrent of manuscripts produced in the Middle Ages, only a few are scrolls. If we set all the literary (that is, not record-keeping) codices against all the literary scrolls, the codices might outnumber the scrolls by a thousand to one. But if we add in all the notarial, record-keeping, legal, and other archival volumes, the numbers might come out much closer to even, owing to the medieval habit, especially in England, of keeping records on scrolls.

The surviving medieval scrolls are fascinating for what they tell us about the special circumstances that provoked this format. We will look at the people who made them and the objects—some of them ugly and worn, others grand and magnificent—that continued the ancient practice of writing on scrolls.

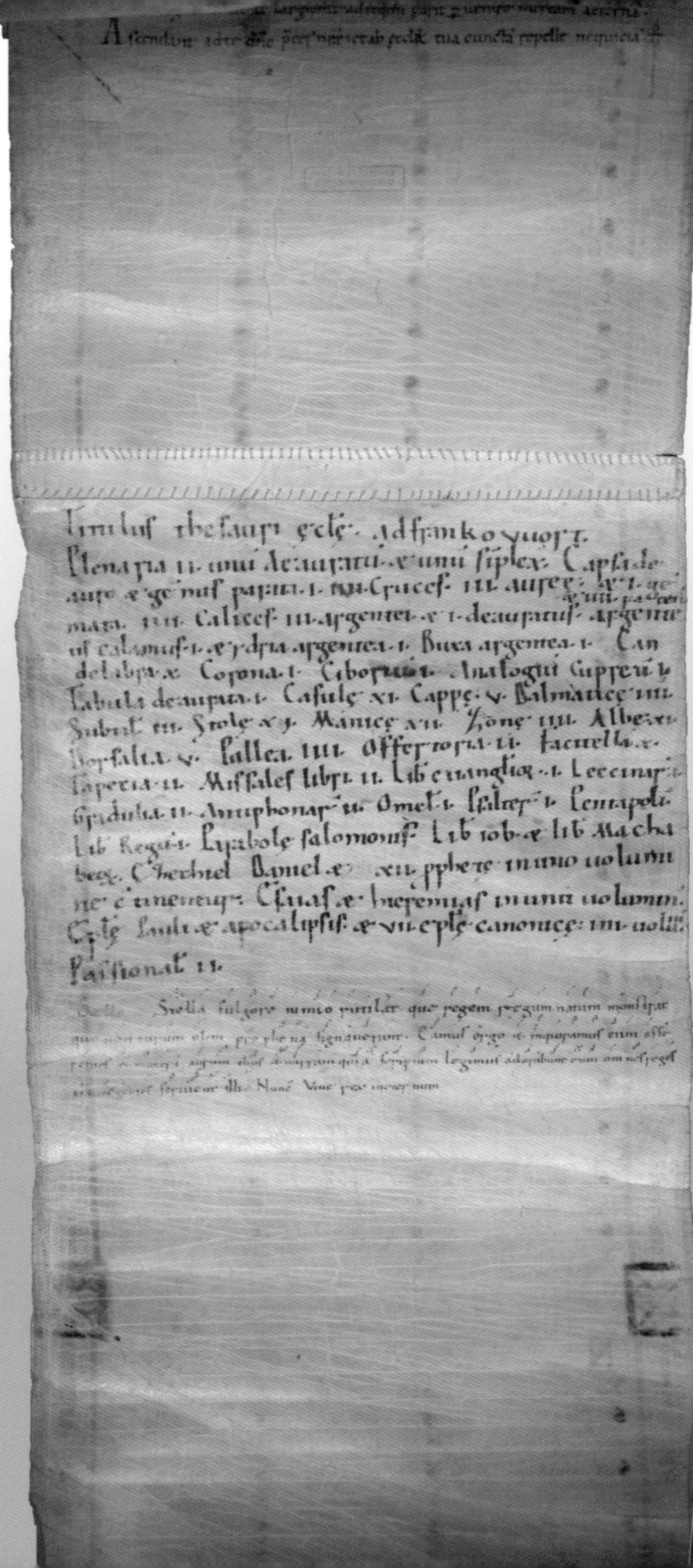

Titulus thesauri eccle. ad franko uuort.
Plenaria ii. unu deauratu. e unu siplex. Capsi de
auro e ege nus papiu. i. tu Cruces. iii. aurec. x. i. ge
mata. iiii. Calices iii. argentei. e i. deauratus. argente
us calamus. i. e. dria argentea. i. Buxa argemea. i. Can
delabra x. Corona. i. Ciborium. Analogiu cupreu i.
Tabula deaurata. i. Casule xi. Cappe. v. Dalmatice iiii.
Subtil. iii. Stole x. i. Manice xii. Zone iiii. Albe x.
bor salia. v. Pallea iiii. Offertoria ii. Facitella. e.
Coperia ii. Missales libri ii. Lib euangliou. i. Lec ciiii.
Gradula ii. Antiphonar. ii. Omei. i. Psalter. i. Pentapoli.
Lib Regu. i. Parabole salomonis. Lib iob. e lib Macha
beor. Ezechiel Daniel. e xii pphere in uno uolumi
ne e tenentur. Esaias. e. Ieremias in una uolumi.
Eple Pauli. e apocalipsis. e vii eple canonice. in uolii.
Passional ii.

Stella fulgore nimio simile que regem regum natum monstrat
que uota ununi olim pro plena signauerunt. Camus ergo e inquiramus enim offe
remus e munera aurum thus demirram qui a scripturam legimus adorabur eum om nes reges
in cludit seruire illi. Nunc. Vine per mener num

FIG. 1.1
A joint between
two membranes of a
scroll. In this case, the
overlap is closed with
a double stitching with
thread. The scroll itself
shows the dorse (back)
of the famous ninth-
century Lorsch litany
scroll (see fig. 6.4),
giving an eleventh-
century list of the
treasures of the abbey.
Frankfurt am Main,
Universitätsbibliothek
Johann Christian
Senckenberg, MS
Barth 179.

What Is a Scroll?

A scroll, otherwise known as a rotulus or roll, is a length of papyrus, leather, or parchment, on which writing, drawing, or painting is preserved, and which is stored in a rolled form. Scrolls are most often made by fastening together, with glue, thread, or thongs, several separate pieces, or membranes, to make a scroll of some length. Scrolls are usually wound around a central baton, the umbilicus. Because of this, the papyrus, parchment, or leather that is nearest the center generally receives far less wear than the outer portions even though it might bear the weight of the whole length of the scroll, especially since the outer membranes must be handled at every use in reaching the center.

Scrolls are oriented either horizontally or vertically. The writing is sometimes arranged in a series of columns written from top to bottom of the width, so the scroll is held sideways for reading and writing. This layout is almost universal in scrolls from ancient Greece and Rome, and is also used for Hebrew scrolls. (It is of course very rare for a horizontal scroll to be written in long lines across the entire long dimension. Think about it.) Chinese scrolls start from the right, and are read in a series of individual columns of characters. Most Western medieval scrolls, though, are oriented vertically, written from top to bottom, usually in a single continuous column of text, which may be interrupted by diagrams or illustrations. This is the arrangement familiar to most of us from texts on our computer screens.

Like movies on film, which must be rewound, scrolls must be rerolled after use. Continuous use causes uneven wear, especially at the beginning of a scroll. Sometimes a blank sheet, or a strip of cloth or leather, is attached to the beginning to wrap and protect the scroll when it has been rolled.

Most of the terms now generally used for books were at first applied to scrolls exclusively, since the scroll was for many centuries the standard way to preserve writing. The Greek term *chartes* (Latin *charta*, which becomes both "paper"—*carta* in Italian—and "charter") refers both to writing material and to its rolled form. The Greek *byblos* or *biblos* comes

FIG. 1.2
A scroll rolled on its umbilicus. This scroll, the
second *Exultet* of Montecassino (see fig. 6.10,
p. 163), has been restored; its umbilicus is not
original. Montecassino, Archivio dell'Abbazia,
Exultet 2. Photo Giulio Menna.

from the ancient Mediterranean city from which papyrus was first imported; the name, and its diminutive, *biblion* (hence "bible"), came to mean both papyrus and the book in its rolled form.

More specific terms are Greek *kilindros* (hence "cylinder") and Latin *volumen* (hence "volume"), which refer specifically to the shape of the roll rather than to its material. Longer texts often had to be written on several scrolls, which would be read successively, *volumen* by *volumen*.

A *tomos* ("tome") in its original sense is a cutting (from Greek *temno*, to cut) from a *volumen*, hence a portion of a larger roll. Later, tome came to mean a part of a larger work and, ultimately, a book in itself.

Saint Jerome, the fourth-century translator of the Latin Bible, uses the words *liber* and *volumen*, seemingly interchangeably, to describe longer texts written on several scrolls. Apparently he uses *liber* when he is thinking of the work being transmitted, and *volumen* when he thinks of the material. Thus, several *libri* can be contained in one *volumen*. Jerome does seem to mean a scroll when he says *volumen*, and he refers especially to Hebrew scriptures as being *volumina*.

The term "rotulus" was a later Latin coinage for a rolled document, and is used in many other languages (for example, *rotolo, roule, rouleau, rodillo, rodel, rôle*, roll). The word "scroll" is from Middle English *scrowle*, influenced by *rowle*, a roll.

Scrolls in Asia and Africa

We know that scrolls have been made and used for five thousand years, although the oldest surviving scrolls are from about 2500 BCE. In 2015, a joint French-Egyptian team of archaeologists led by Pierre Tallet announced the discovery at Wadi-al-Jarf, near the Red Sea, of a trove of papyrus fragments that included the diary of Merer, an Egyptian official involved in the building of the great pyramid of the Pharoah Khufu (2589–2566 BCE). He was in charge of moving stone, by boat, to Giza. These are, for now, the oldest known surviving scrolls.

✥ SOUTH ASIA

The sutra scroll, used across Asia, could be called the progenitor of all other types of Asian scroll that were originally for religious texts. *Sutra* means "string" or "thread," and came to mean an aphorism or a collection of sayings; the term is used in Hindu and Buddhist contexts. Folded in a zigzag, like an accordion, sutra scrolls have the advantage of giving easy access to any place on the scroll, even though the scroll must be creased. (An accordion-folded document is perhaps not really a scroll, but sutra scrolls are often rolled rather than folded.)

By the fourth century BCE, scrolls were used in India, mostly for religious texts, and the tradition continues today on the Indian subcontinent, including Nepal, Bangladesh, Tibet, and other areas. Long narrative scrolls are stored rolled and brought out for display in temples on special occasions. Smaller hanging scrolls, called *tangka*, depict the Buddha and Buddhist themes. Pata painting (or patachitra, "painting on cloth") is a sort of religious folk art that appears on long cloths, often folded rather than rolled.

Only very recently have several hundred fragments of Buddhist manuscripts been discovered in eastern Afghanistan and northern Pakistan. These include some of the oldest surviving texts in any Indian or Buddhist language. Some of them date back to the first century BCE, when Buddhist texts were first written down. The earlier manuscripts were birch-bark scrolls, but within a few centuries the Buddhists there seem to have adopted the palm-leaf folio format (pothī) that prevails in the rest of India.

The spread of Buddhism brought scrolls to China by the first century CE, and from there to Japan several centuries later. In fact, the scroll was the standard format for recording texts in China until about the eleventh century CE, when the codex supplanted it.

✤ CHINA

Long scrolls, oriented horizontally, were used in China to illustrate, with painting and text, events, geography, and other suitable subjects; they are meant to be viewed gradually as they are unrolled, usually from right to left. Among the most priceless of these works are the Southern Inspection Tour scrolls documenting the visit of Kangxi, emperor of China, to inspect his southern provinces, including a traditional visit to Mount Tai.

Kangxi was the longest-reigning emperor in Chinese history (about 1654–1722). The fourth of the Manchu-led Qing dynasty, he was a powerful military leader, and brought about a period of prosperity and stability. He oversaw the production of a dictionary of Chinese characters, and a collection of Tang poetry. His interest in Western culture and technology supported Jesuit missionaries, and it was his Western court musician who taught him to play the spinet.

The emperor's tour is illustrated on a series of twelve scrolls. Taken together, they are some nine hundred feet long, and covered with spectacular illustrations of the emperor, his retinue, and the sites visited in the course of his tour.

Smaller hanging scrolls are often used to display calligraphy. Chinese calligraphic scrolls, objects of beauty in which a text combines meaning and visual beauty, are hung vertically on the wall. They are usually painted on paper or silk, and sometimes mounted with decorative borders. They are meant for temporary display, and are otherwise stored rolled up.

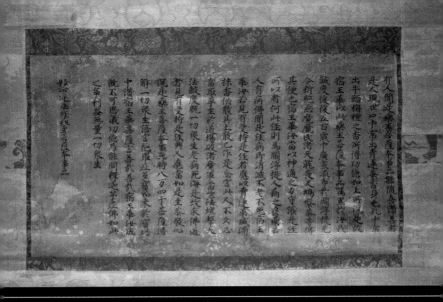

FIG. I.3A

A twelfth-century scroll containing a part of the Lotus sutra, one of the Buddhist texts brought to Japan, showing "The Former Deeds of Bodhisattva Medicine King," chapter 23 of the Lotus sutra (*Hokekyô*). This beautiful example of a sutra scroll is currently displayed as a hanging scroll, but was originally part of a set of horizontal handscrolls. This left-most scroll contains the title at the left end. Delicately painted lotus plants line the upper and lower edges of the scroll. Ink on dyed paper decorated with ink, color, silver pigment, scattered gold- and silver leaf, and cut-gold ruled lines; handscroll fragment only: 9 ¹³/₁₆ × 17 ⁵/₁₆ in. (25 × 44 cm); mounting, including cord and roller ends: 43 × 25 in. (109.2 × 63.5 cm). Harvard Art Museums/Arthur M. Sackler Museum, Gift of Mrs. Donald F. Hyde, 1977.202 Photo: Imaging Department © President and Fellows of Harvard College

FIG. I.3B

This seventeenth-century sutra scroll was commissioned by Retired Emperor Gomizunoo (1596–1680) in memory of the Shogun Tokugawa Ieyasu. It contains "The Former Deeds of King Wondrous Splendor," chapter 27 of the Lotus sutra, written by the artist Tosa Mitsuoki (1617–1691). Handscroll; gold and silver on indigo-dyed paper; 11 ¹¹/₁₆ × 106 ⁹/₁₆ in. (29.7 × 270.7 cm). Harvard Art Museums/Arthur M. Sackler Museum, Bequest of the Hofer Collection of the Arts of Asia, 1985.520 Photo: Imaging Department © President and Fellows of Harvard College

FIG. I.4

A detail from scroll 6 of the Southern Inspection Tour of the Quianlong Emperor of China in 1751. Here the emperor enters the city of Suzhou, an important commercial center on the Grand Canal linking northern and southern China. The scroll from which this small detail is reproduced, dated 1770, is one of twelve scrolls painted by the artist Xu Yang, documenting this tour. Four such scrolls have been digitized, and can be viewed at http://www.learn.columbia.edu/nanxuntu/start.html. Handscroll; ink and color on silk, 27⅛ × 784½ in. (68.8 × 1994 cm). Purchase, The Dillon Fund Gift, 1988 (1988.350a-d). Image copyright© The Metropolitan Museum of Art. Image source: Art Resource, NY.

FIG. I.5

Moon and Melon, 1689. A Chinese hanging scroll combining calligraphy and painting, executed by Zhu Da (also known as Bada Shanren), 1626–1706, one of the most influential artists of his period. Living in Buddhist monasteries at a time of great conflict at the end of the Ming dynasty, he spent a quiet life of Buddhist teaching, poetry, and painting and calligraphy.

The poem on the scroll, as translated by Richard M. Barnhart, reads:

> A Ming cake seen from one side,
> The moon, so round when the melons rise.
> Everyone points to the mooncakes,
> But hope that the melons will ripen is a fool's dream.

Hanging scroll: ink on paper; with signature "Bada Shanren"; painting proper: 29 × 17¾ in.; mounting, including cord and roller ends: 82½ × 25¾ in. Harvard Art Museums/Arthur M. Sackler Museum, Gift of Earl Morse, Harvard Law School, Class of 1930, 1964.94 Photo: Imaging Department © President and Fellows of Harvard College.

❖ JAPAN

The Japanese *kakejiku* or *kakemono* is a similar kind of calligraphic scroll. It is often mounted on a background of silk or other fabric, and is intended to be displayed hanging on a wall. The Japanese *emakimono*, or *emaki*, are narrative scrolls, with pictures and text. Read from right to left; they are rerolled at the right as they are unrolled from the roller at the left. They may deal with aspects of court life, religion, folk tales, or even convey romantic themes. Usually they begin with explanatory text, followed by a series of painted narrative scenes; sometimes the text alternates with the pictures, as in an illustrated book. They are in a way forerunners of Japanese manga, Western comic books, and graphic novels, although they are seldom meant to be funny. Some are intended for women; these have a particular pictorial style and tend to depict romance and aspects of court life. Others, intended for men, have historical subjects, with a particular preference for descriptions of battles.

Among the most famous *emaki* is *The Tale of Genji*, from about 1130, an extensive narrative written by the noblewoman Morisak Shikibu, illustrating the life and adventures of the son of an ancient emperor. Early versions of the text were often folded accordion-style rather than rolled.

❖ KOREA

In Korea, there is a very beautiful and very large Buddhist hanging scroll that depicts the bodhisattva Avalokiteshvara, another pan-Asian Buddhist subject. Such scrolls are scrolls only by tradition, since such precious objects do not look as though they are meant to be rolled, but instead to be displayed hanging.

FIG. 1.6
Korean Buddhist scroll. This fourteenth-century hanging scroll is one of the largest extant paintings from the Koryŏ dynasty (918–1392). It depicts the meeting of the pious youth Sudhana, the tiny figure at lower left, and Avalokiteshvara, the Bodhisattva of Compassion. Hanging scroll; ink, color, and gold pigment on silk; painting proper: 62¹³⁄₁₆ × 32½ in. (159.6 × 82.5 cm); mounting, including cord and roller ends: 108 × 45 in. (274.3 × 114.3 cm). Harvard Art Museums/Arthur M. Sackler Museum, Bequest of Grenville L. Winthrop, 1943.57.12 Photo: Imaging Department © President and Fellows of Harvard College.

The Middle East

A discovery of almost a thousand scrolls was made during the 1940s and 1950s at Khirbet Qumran in the West Bank. Often referred to as the Dead Sea Scrolls, these contributed enormously to our understanding of religious history. Their number indicates that scrolls were the normal way of conveying a text around the Mediterranean in the Second Temple Period, 530 BCE –70 CE.

Hebrew and Aramaic scrolls have been utilized for thousands of years, and the Torah, the scroll of the Five Books of Moses, continues to be an indispensable part of Jewish worship. The oldest surviving Torah scroll is one, now in Bologna, dating from the twelfth or thirteenth century CE.

The Book of Esther, commonly written on a scroll called a megillah, is read at the feast of Purim. The word "megillah" comes from an early rabbinical commentary on the book of Esther, and has come to mean a well-formed text—or, in other words, a scroll. (The expression "the whole megillah" means an overcomplicated explanation.) Copies of the Torah and the megillah continue to be manufactured today, by scribes and craftsmen whose techniques in many ways preserve those of the medieval artists who created the scrolls that are the subject of this book.

✤ ARABIC SCROLLS

Arabic scrolls with calligraphic Qur'anic verses survive from as early as the fourteenth century, although most copies of the Qur'an are in codex form. Paper scrolls are used in the Muslim world for amulets (including prayers and verses from the Qur'an), and for certificates attesting that a devout Muslim has completed the Hajj pilgrimage to Mecca. Some of these certificates are beautifully decorated. Both parchment and paper are used for calendar scrolls.

A fascinating phenomenon, indicating the extent of Arabic influence, is the *aljamía* texts of El-Andalus, the Islamic part of what is now Spain. Many religious and other types of texts were translated into Spanish but written using the Arabic alphabet. This tradition (*aljamía* is Arabic for

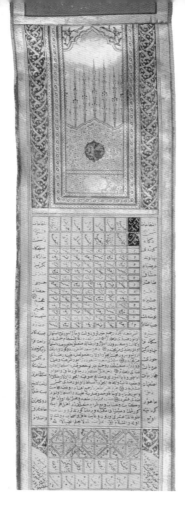

FIG 1.7

An Ottoman *rûzname* (book of days), a set of calendar tables in the Islamic and Rumi calendars, along with other useful information. Functioning as a portable almanac, it includes texts describing the stations of the sun and moon, the musical modes, the Muslim calendar, the times of prayer in different seasons, and the times of sunrise and sunset—all arranged according to the position of Istanbul. A leather flap at the beginning is meant to wrap around and protect the scroll when rolled.

After the decorative headpiece (*serlevha*) shown here, a table shows the hours of the day and the night, with their ruling planets in the center; on the left and right the planets are enumerated along with appropriate musical modes. Various grids make up the rest of the scroll, accompanied by explanatory text in Ottoman Turkish alongside the grids in the margins.

The painted and gilded scroll on parchment is signed by Katib Muhammad Ma'aruf Na'ili and dated 1810. Attributed to Turkey. Ink, opaque watercolor, and gold on parchment; 4 × 41 in. (10.2 × 104 cm). Louis E. and Theresa S. Seley Purchase Fund for Islamic Art, 1990 (1990.265). The Metropolitan Museum of Art, New York, NY, U.S.A. Image copyright © The Metropolitan Museum of Art. Image source: Art Resource, NY.

"non-Arab language") continued during the persecution of the Muslims, and when King Philip II outlawed the use of Arabic in 1526, the creation and clandestine circulation of aljamía scrolls was a principal means of keeping Morisco culture alive. Most of the surviving scrolls are in the National Library of Spain.

Ethiopia

Among the Christians of Ethiopia, scrolls used for healing and for warding off evil spirits are manufactured by *däbtäras*, unordained priests of the Ethiopian church. Scrolls are made to order, often the length of a

FIG. 1.8

An Ethiopian magic scroll. This type of scroll is commissioned and owned by an individual to invoke prayers for recovery from an illness or another need. Such scrolls are made by Christian clerics, but not as part of their official duties; the scrolls often contain magical spells that are not fully orthodox. Magic scrolls are often made to the length of the person who commissions them so they can be laid over the body to aid in healing. The commissioner of this scroll, to judge from its length, stood 5 feet 2 inches tall. When not in use these scrolls are often displayed hanging on a wall or stored rolled in a pouch. New Haven, Beinecke Rare Book and Manuscript Library Ethiopic MSS 28.

client's body (so that they can be stretched out on the client for healing), and are sometimes longer if the scroll is intended for a household—in which case it can be displayed hanging.

There is an understanding that the animal whose hide is used for the parchment substitutes, in a way, for the client. The priest writes his texts in Ge'ez, the language of the church, in red and black. There are biblical and liturgical passages, spells that ward off the evil eye, and spells for healing. Many of these texts call on God, on the Virgin Mary, and on other saints. The client's name is added to the scroll last. Scrolls are often decorated with talismanic designs of great beauty. When they are not being used, magic scrolls are stored in red leather tubular cases with a cap. The fact that these scrolls include magic spells, and that they are used as talismans or amulets, explains why they are not an official part of the religious practice of the Ethiopian church.

Scrolls in Ancient Egypt, Greece, and Rome

The medieval Latin West drew its literary heritage largely from that of ancient Rome, where the scroll had been the standard way of recording a text. The Romans had taken it over from the Greeks, and both cultures relied on papyrus from Egypt for their writing materials. So, we must begin in ancient Egypt.

✦ EGYPT

Papyrus scrolls were standard in ancient Egypt, used for almost all kinds of writing. Papyrus sheets, made from plant fibers, were glued end to end to make long scrolls. Papyrus, which gives its name to paper, was essentially an exclusive product of Egypt, since the plant was cultivated along the Nile. It was an important and valuable commodity, and the export of papyrus sheets and scrolls made possible the writing of almost everything that survives of the literature of Egypt, Greece, and Rome.

There's an extensive description of how to make papyrus sheets in the *Natural History* of Pliny the Elder, who wrote about, well, everything, in the first century CE. (He died trying to observe the eruption of Vesuvius.) He wrote:

> Before passing from Egypt, something should be said with regard to papyrus, since in the use of this material the culture and history of mankind are preeminently embodied. . . .
>
> It grows in the marshes of Egypt and in the stagnant waters of the inundations of the Nile. . . . Its root has the thickness of a man's arm, with a triangular section. Its height is not more than ten cubits, ending in a feathery top, like a thyrsus [a staff topped with a pine cone]. . . .

And he goes on to describe, in almost painful detail, how the sheets are first made, and then how those sheets are made into scrolls:

> The method of preparation of the writing material from papyrus is as follows. It is divided with a needle into strips, exceedingly thin but as wide as possible. The best quality is provided by the strips from the middle [of the stem], the next to these following in order of merit . . . [here Pliny describes and names the various qualities of papyrus, starting with Augusta, named for the emperor . . .]
>
> The sheets are soaked during the process of fabrication in Nile water; for this turbid fluid has the effect of glue. A layer is first laid out on a flat board of the width for which the papyrus-fibres [parallel in a single direction] suffice. Its edges are trimmed, and then another layer is superimposed at right angles to it. It is then pressed in a pressing-machine, the sheets are dried in the sun, and are then attached to one another, the qualities being arranged in descending order of merit. There are never more than twenty sheets in a roll. The best qualities have a width of 13 digits [about 9¾ in.]. . . .

Sheets of papyrus, Pliny says, varied by size and quality, but they average something like ten inches high. The sheets, about seven or eight inches wide, are glued together to make a continuous sideways scroll. Pliny says that rolls are not longer than twenty sheets, but that does not

FIG. 1.9

A portion of an Egyptian *Book of the Dead*, often called *Book of Coming Forth into the Daylight*. This is the third sheet of the papyrus of Ani, dating from the Nineteenth Dynasty (ca. 1250 BCE). The scene is the hall of judgment; in the center is a balance holding a feather (right) and Ani's heart (left). The little monkey on top of the scale is a form of the god Thoth. The kneeling figure with the head of a jackal is the god Anubis, who steadies the balance.

To the right is another Thoth, this time in human form with a bird's head; he is the scribe who will record the results of this trial. Behind him is an animal ready to spring if Ani's heart should be found wanting.

Ani and his wife Tutu enter the scene from the left to be judged; he speaks a spell from the *Book of the Dead*. Above the scene a row of Egyptian deities look on from their thrones.

mean that all books are twenty sheets wide; another roll could simply be added on, or the roll shortened to match the length of the text.

One such text was *The Egyptian Book of the Dead* (or *Book of Coming Forth into the Daylight*). It was often buried with a dead person, along with other useful materials to aid the transition from life to death. Copies of this book, usually illustrated, are known to come from as early as about 1500 BCE. Its text is not fixed, but it often includes depictions of gods and of the deceased.

✤ GREECE AND ROME

Ready-made rolls of Egyptian papyrus, as Pliny describes, were regularly available for sale, and they were the basis for literary scrolls in Greece and Rome. Romans and Greeks read to each other using scrolls, and scrolls were part of the fabric of civic and private life. The Ionic capitals used in columns in both Greece and Rome resemble a scroll partially opened, and their scrolled volutes are so named from a Latin word for unrolling a scroll.

FIG. I.10

A Greek physician studies a scroll; on a chest sits a codex, below which a number of scrolls are stored. A Roman sarcophagus with a Greek Physician, Late Roman (fourth century CE). An inscription in Greek reads: "If anyone shall dare to bury another person along with this one, he shall pay to the treasury three times two thousand [whatever the unit was]. This is what he shall pay to [the city of] Portus, but he himself will endure the eternal punishment of the violator of graves. Marble, 21¾ × 23¼ × 84⅞ in. (55.2 × 59.1 × 215.6 cm). Gift of Mrs. Joseph Brummer and Ernest Brummer, in memory of Joseph Brummer, 1948 (48. 76.1). Image copyright © The Metropolitan Museum of Art. Image source: Art Resource, NY.

Greek scrolls, and Roman ones after them, were held sideways and written in a series of columns, about three inches wide, that go from the top to the bottom of the short dimension of the scroll; to us an unfurled scroll looks like a series of book pages written one after another from left to right. Whereas some Egyptian scrolls were very long—reaching a hundred feet or more when they were versions of the *Book of the Dead*—Greek scrolls seldom reach twenty-five feet in length. It seems clear that the scrolls were assembled before writing, since the columns are often written over the glued joints between sheets of papyrus. (Furthermore, we know from Pliny that papyrus was assembled in rolls before reaching the market.)

A Roman scroll, like a Greek one, might be seven to ten inches high and about thirty feet long, and was usually written in a series of *paginae*, or columns. Scrolls often began with a blank column to protect the written text when the scroll was handled. The title (the index or *titulus*) might be written on a strip-like label attached to the outside of the scroll; at the end of the scroll there might be a colophon, giving information about the book and its author, the scribe, the owner, and the date. So our present terminology of page, volume, tome, title, and colophon all derive from the Roman scroll form.

Sometimes scrolls, especially larger or more important ones, were attached to batons at either end, making them easier to hold. These are mentioned in literary references, though no ancient batons survive.

Scrolls were often, but not always, written on one side only, for reasons of convenience and concern for the text being written. An opisthographic roll is one written on both sides, either originally or in the process of reusing the blank outer side of an older scroll. Writing on the back of a scroll was a matter of expediency or thrift; a literary scroll for sale in the ancient world would be written on the front only. This is partly because the outside of the papyrus scroll is the layer with vertical fibers (remember Pliny says that a papyrus sheet is made of two layers at right angles), which are prone to stretching and abrasion when rolled, so that writing on the outside is risky. The work of Pliny the Elder was an exception; his nephew, known as Pliny the Younger, reports that the elder Pliny left 160 volumes written front and back in a very small hand—he was saving papyrus.

Scrolls can contain a great deal, however, if we believe the report of the Byzantine historian Zonaras, who claimed that the great library of 120,000 books at Constantinople included a scroll 120 feet long, made from the intestine of a serpent, which contained the *Iliad* and the *Odyssey* written in letters of gold.

Scrolls can be damaged by being squashed or flattened, so Romans and Greeks often stored them upright in a book box (*capsa*), horizontally on a shelf, or in a pigeonhole. Particularly valuable scrolls could be placed in a chest or wrapped in a protective sleeve of parchment and tied with thongs. A single long work, like Virgil's *Aeneid*, very often required several scrolls, which would be kept in the same book box. It was these physical limitations—the length of the papyrus scroll and the number of scrolls that could be stored together—that tended to define the subdivisions of longer works of literature. A long work like an epic poem would be divided into books (or tomes, or *volumina*), each on its own scroll, and the whole collection of volumes stored together in a *capsa*.

Greek and Roman rolls might seem to us hard to read. They are usually labeled at the end, so unless there's a tab, you can't tell what the title is until you've read the text all the way through. The text is not generally separated into words, and it lacks much in the way of punctuation. It must have been impossible to make reference to a particular place in a book, and long texts had to be divided among several scrolls. You have to rewind a scroll after reading, and that requires two hands; it may unroll if you drop it. It may not seem an ideal system. And yet, you might prefer, say, to read one book of the *Aeneid* at a time; and if you are a member of the literate leisured class and can afford books, you probably have servants to roll them back up.

Frederic G. Kenyon, director of the British Museum and the author of the classic *Books and Readers in Ancient Greece and Rome* (1932) noted these problems when he wrote, "It cannot be denied that throughout the classical period the technique of book-production left something to be desired, and that the convenience of the reader was little consulted."

FIG. 1.11

A Roman sarcophagus. A seated figure reads from
a scroll and gestures to Thalia, the muse of comedy.

For example, Pliny the Younger tells of Verginius Rufus, a powerful Roman commander who had been born in Pliny's home town of Comum (Como). Verginius was consul under the emperor Nero, and governor of the province of Upper Germany. Twice he refused the offer of the emperorship; coming out of retirement to serve the emperor Nerva, he bent down to retrieve a scroll he had dropped, fell over, broke his hip, and died of complications.

Famous libraries in Pergamum, Alexandria, Rome, and elsewhere were designed to accommodate the storage of scrolls. The great library

FIG. 1.12

A copy of the statue of Sophocles in the Lateran Palace, Rome. A *capsa*, or scroll case, is at the poet's feet; it contains a number of scrolls, stored upright. Cast by P. P. Caproni, George Walter Vincent Smith Art Museum, Springfield, Massachusetts. The Horace Smith Collection. Photography by John Polak.

of Trajan in Rome was divided into Latin and Greek sections. Shelves for books, called *pegmata*, had hollow sections called *nidi* (Latin for nests), which were further divided into a sort of honeycomb structure with individual hollows called *foruli* or *locumenta* (little holes or places), each designed to hold a single closed scroll. These libraries were meant for storage, not for study; reading was normally done out of doors, and sometimes as public events. Tables for reading in libraries seem to have arrived in the Middle Ages alongside the codex.

✠ SURVIVING ANCIENT SCROLLS

Very few scrolls survive from classical civilization. Papyrus, being organic, tends to decay in the presence of moisture, and the many scrolls that we see in carvings and pictures represent something that is essentially lost to us. The texts that we do have from Greece and Rome mostly date from the Middle Ages, and are copies that were made by monks, clerics, and scholars of older copies, which themselves were copies. But they are not scrolls.

Two large collections of ancient scrolls owe their amazing and fortunate survival to unusual climatic conditions.

Near ancient Oxyrhynchus, in Egypt (modern-day el-Bahnasa), an ancient garbage dump excavated, beginning in 1896, by the archaeologists Bernard Pyne Grenfell and Arthur Surridge Hunt revealed a stash of thousands of ancient papyrus scrolls and fragments, along with a few written on parchment. The dry climate of Egypt and the protection of being buried preserved these scrolls better than any other group of ancient texts. Beginning at the end of the nineteenth century, hundreds of scrolls dating from the first to the sixth century revealed texts of Greek literature, Jewish and Christian biblical texts, and much else. Most of the surviving documents are fragments, and most of them are letters, lists, and record-keeping documents, but the group still provides some enormously important biblical texts and fills in a few gaps in our knowledge of Greek literature.

Many of the Oxyrhynchus papyri are at the Ashmolean Museum

at Oxford (Grenfell's home institution), but others are scattered all over the world. They have been edited in a huge series of volumes that is now available online (http://www.papyrology.ox.ac.uk/POxy/).

The other major survival is that found in the so-called Villa of the Papyri in Herculaneum, the city destroyed—much like Pompeii—in the eruption of Vesuvius in 79 CE. The villa may have belonged to Julius Caesar's father-in-law, Lucius Calpurnius Piso Caesoninus. (The villa itself is the model for the Getty Villa in California, where an idea of the luxury and beauty of the original house can be understood.) In 1754, excavators found a small room, about twelve feet square, containing hundreds of scrolls in ornamental bookcases around the room, with a table in the center. They had unearthed the only surviving library from the classical world. Everything was essentially charred to cinders, the books resembling sticks of charcoal.

The history of these papyri is a story in itself. The king of Naples, Ferdinand IV, presented six scrolls to Napoleon Bonaparte in 1802 as a diplomatic offering. Napoleon in turn gave them to the Institut de France, where they remain today. Ferdinand gave eighteen papyri to King George IV of England in 1810; they are now in the Bodleian and the British Library. Most of the rest of the scrolls that have been excavated so far are in the Naples Archaeological Museum.

Nobody has yet discovered a way to unroll and read one of these scrolls without destroying it at the same time. Father Antonio Piaggio, a conservator at the Vatican in the late eighteenth century, invented a machine for unrolling a scroll: silk threads were used to separate the outer layer of the scroll. As the machine turned, fragments of the roll broke off like tree bark and fell onto glued paper. Transcribers immediately wrote down what they could see, before the fragments became illegible. The process was very slow—the first scroll took about four years to unroll—and it was very destructive.

The English clergyman John Hayter (1756–1818), funded by the Prince of Wales, continued the work of unrolling and transcribing. About two hundred scrolls were unrolled, and half of them transcribed in pencil facsimiles, but because the process of unrolling destroys the

ΤΗΤΑΠΕΙΝΟΥΟΛΑΠΟΥΟΤΙ
ΩΣΑΝΘΟΣΧΟΡΤΟΥΠΑΡΕ
ΛΕΥΣΕΤΑΙΑΝΕΤΕΙΛΕΝΓΑΡ
ΟΗΥΟΣΣΥΝΤΩΚΑΥΣΩΝΕΙ
ΚΑΙΕΞΗΡΑΝΕΝΤΟΝΧΟΡΤΟ
ΚΑΙΤΟΑΝΘΟΣΑΥΤΟΥΕΞΕΠΕ
ΣΕΝΚΑΙΗΕΥΠΡΕΠΕΙΑΤΟΥΠΡΟΣΩ
ΠΟΥΑΥΤΟΥΑΠΩΛΕΤΟΟΥ
ΤΩΣΚΑΙΟΠΛΟΥΣΙΟΣΕΝΤΑΙΣ
ΠΟΡΕΙΑΙΣΑΥΤΟΥΜΑΡΑΝ
ΘΗΣΕΤΑΙΜΑΚΑΡΙΟΣΑΝΗ
ΡΟΣΥΠΟΜΕΝΕΙΠΕΙΡΑ
ΣΜΟΝΟΤΙΔΟΚΙΜΟΣΓΕΝΟ
ΜΕΝΟΣΛΗΜΨΕΤΑΙΤΟΝ
ΣΤΕΦΑΝΟΝΤΗΣΖΩΗΣ

scroll, to know its text meant to lose it. So we have some idea of the contents of the library, but not much, because so far, the more we know, the more we destroy.

From what has been deciphered, this Herculaneum library seems to be a rather specialized Greek collection of Epicurean texts, some by Epicurus himself, others by some of his followers. A lot of the texts are by Philodemus of Gadara, who lived in Herculaneum and may have had a part in selecting the contents of the library. It is not, unfortunately, a library full of lost classics.

There are nearly two thousand scrolls and fragments; more remain to be excavated. Modern archaeologists have attempted various methods to decipher them, including multispectral imaging, nuclear magnetic resonance, and X-ray tomography. The work might not be so difficult if the scrolls were uniformly circular and the layers uniformly thick, but the charred remains are often fused, and they have bulges, wrinkles, and other irregularities. X-ray tomography cannot distinguish between the carbon of charred papyrus and carbon-based ink, unfortunately.

But on September 22, 2016, the *New York Times* announced that a charred scroll from about 100 CE in En-Gedi, Israel, had been deciphered. It was virtually unrolled and read by a new three-dimensional reconstruction technique developed by Dr. W. Brent Seales of the University of Kentucky. Dr. Seales, who also worked on two of the Napoleon scrolls in Paris, calls his technique "virtual unwrapping," since it permits the display in two dimensions of a virtual object scanned in three dimensions. The scroll in the news contains a portion of the Masoretic text of the Book of Leviticus, concerning, appropriately enough, burnt offerings! And Dr. Vito Mocella of the National Research Council in Rome has recently said that experiments have shown that x-ray phase contrast tomography technique can detect the text within the scrolls of Herculaneum.

FIG. 1.13

(*Opposite*) Oxyrhynchus Papyrus no. 1229; an excerpt, written in the early third century CE, from the Epistle of James, in Greek. Courtesy of The Spurlock Museum, University of Illinois at Urbana-Champaign.

We can hope that the remainder of the library of the Villa of the Papyri will now be unearthed, scanned, virtually unwrapped, and added to our knowledge of classical civilization.

Scroll and Codex

In Greece and Rome, literature was written on scrolls. For lesser texts, tablets made of wood or bark could be used for lists, letters, and other less exalted things. If you fold a piece of parchment in two or four (making a booklet of four or eight pages), you can use it instead of a wooden tablet for writing. And it is just such folded pocket books that ultimately replaced the scroll; if you stack several of them up, and bind them together, you have a codex, just like the print version of this book.

By the fourth century CE, the codex was the preferred medium for all kinds of writing in the Latin West, and became the standard support for texts from then on. Parchment, rather than papyrus, was the usual material for making a codex, and the transition to parchment, about which little is actually known, was directly related to the change of format.

The codex format arrived with Christianity, but scholars disagree on whether the one is dependent on the other. Christian texts are almost always codices, not scrolls. But that does not mean that early codices were mostly Christian, or that Christians were responsible for the introduction of the codex. Traditional explanations note that a small codex can contain all the gospels, and can be hidden under a toga, but in fact most early Christian books contain a single gospel, not all four.

Early codices were not luxury products, but they have obvious advantages: easy reference to any part of the text, relatively uniform wear (remember, the outer parts of a scroll always wear out first), and the ability to include more text in a smaller space. Pope Gregory the Great noted that within the space of six codices he had fit a work that had occupied thirty-five scrolls.

The arrival of the codex, whatever the reasons for the transition, was a moment of great technical importance, and the form of the codex has been with us ever since. The adoption of the codex form and the invention of printing were the two most important developments in the history of communication between the invention of writing and the arrival of electronic media. But scrolls continued to be useful in particular situations, and it is those special scrolls that we pursue here.

Images of Scrolls

Scrolls are often depicted in works of art as the objects they are: texts; thus, the scroll in classical art represents the standard vehicle for a text. But in medieval and later art the scroll may have a particular symbolic significance.

In medieval art, prophets of the Hebrew Bible are represented as holding scrolls, as distinguished from the codices held by evangelists and other Christian writers. This makes sense, since most Hebrew texts were in fact on scrolls, while Christian texts, as noted above, were most often circulated in codices.

In the sixth-century mosaics of San Vitale in Ravenna, the evangelists are depicted with codices (even though two of them, Matthew and Luke, are also depicted with a *capsa* full of scrolls). On the lower walls, the prophets hold scrolls.

In his book about the liturgy, *Rationale divinorum officiorum*, the scholarly bishop Guillaume Durand (d. 1296) wrote, "And note that the patriarchs and prophets are painted with rolls [Durand's word is *rotulis*] in their hands, but some of the apostles with books and some with rolls. Surely because before the advent of Christ the faith was set forth under figures, whereby it was in many aspects not clearly expounded. To show this, the patriarchs and prophets are painted with rolls, to signify that it was, so to say, imperfect knowledge." Clearly Durand is writing in the age of the codex!

FIG. 1.14

In this mosaic of the third century CE, the Roman poet Virgil, seated with a scroll in his lap, is attended by two muses, Clio the muse of history with a scroll, and Melpomene, the muse of tragedy with a tragic mask. Virgil's scroll contains the eighth line of his *Aeneid*, "Musa, mihi causas memora, quo numine laeso" (in Dryden's translation, "O Muse! the causes and the crimes relate"). Bardo Museum, Tunis, Tunisia. Wikimedia Commons. User: Sailko.

FIG. 1.15

Two mosaics from the sixth-century church of San Vitale, Ravenna. Below, the prophet Jeremiah displays his scroll in classical fashion, left to right. The evangelist Saint Luke (above), holds a codex that reads "SECUNDUM LUCAM" (According to Luke); at his feet is a container full of scrolls. San Vitale, Ravenna, Italy/Bridgeman Images; De Agostini Picture Library / A. DeGregorio/Bridgeman Images.

✦ SCROLLS AS SPEECH

In later medieval art, when a codex is depicted it usually represents an actual book: the text of a gospel, the Bible, the Virgin Mary's prayer book. On the other hand, a scroll sometimes represents audible, usually important, speech: the words of angels, of evangelists, of prophets.

In the same way that writing represents language and hence speech, a scroll shown in a painting is a useful way to represent the spoken word. Called by various names, and in a way similar to the balloons in comic strips, the words being spoken by a figure in a painting or sculpture can be represented on a scroll. In an Annunciation scene, the angel Gabriel might appear with a scroll on which is written "Ave Maria" (Hail, Mary), and a similar scroll for the Virgin Mary would probably bear the words of her reply, "Ecce ancilla domini" (Behold the handmaid of the Lord). Many examples exist, including some that may or may not represent speech. (This is not quite the same as the text represented on scrolls—or codices—to identify the character: any figure holding a scroll with the words "In principio erat verbum" (In the beginning was the Word) is a representation of Saint John the Evangelist, whose gospel begins with those words, but not necessarily a picture of him speaking them.

In a side chapel of the church of Abbey Saint-Pierre de Solesmes, France, an ornate sculptural monument depicts a life-size group of figures laying the body of the dead Jesus in the tomb. Above this tableau, in the arches surmounting the scene, two figures hold scrolls with biblical verses. The figures appear to be onlookers who, like a Greek chorus, remind us of how we might react as bystanders.

Scrolls may represent speech, but sometimes they also represent song. In the beautiful glazed terra-cotta of the Nativity (1479) by Andrea della Robbia, God the Father and the Holy Spirit look on as a choir of angels hold up a banner in the form of a scroll, on which is written the text "Gloria in excelsis Deo" (Glory to God in the highest) accompanied by musical notation for one of the most common melodies used when this text is sung at mass. The angels do not need it: they are holding it upside down and backwards from their point of view. The music is there,

FIG. I.16A AND B
Two figures, David and Isaiah, in niches above
the main sculptural scene of the Deposition of
Christ. They comment using Latin biblical texts
("He shall not suffer his holy one to see corruption"
from Psalm 15, and "and his rest shall be glorious,"
Isaiah 11:10). Abbaye Saint-Pierre de Solesmes.

GLORIA IN EXCELS DEO

VERBVM CARO FATTVEST DE VIRGINE M

surely, to give us a visual picture of sound, of what cannot be represented in sculpture. In this way scrolls remained commonplace in pictures even after they were largely obsolete in practice.

Poets are often depicted with scrolls. This is partly because poets frequently used scrolls for their works (more on this below). The beautiful fourteenth-century Manesse codex includes 137 portraits of the poets whose works it includes; two of them can be seen on pages 108 and 109. The scroll is the poet's attribute, and in a sense the scroll represents the poetry as well as the act of reciting it.

Scrolls are not as rare in the world, and in history, as they may seem to be to those of us who do most of our reading in codices. They are widely used in many cultures, and in the West they were for a long time the standard way of representing a text. We ourselves use scrolls every day on the computer. But our understanding of the history of the book is generally simplified in such a way that the fourth-century arrival of the codex in the Latin West marks a sharp and definitive transition. And there are far more codices than scrolls from then onward. But the scrolls that continued to be created, and that survive for our admiration, display a wonderful variety of styles and purposes, all worth exploring for what they tell us about the intentions of those who made and used them. The chapters that follow explore those reasons.

FIG 1.17

(Opposite) A glazed terra-cotta of the Nativity by Andrea della Robbia, 1479. The angels hold a scroll with their music, "Glory to God in the highest," using a familiar melody of Gregorian chant. La Verna, Chiesa Maggiore. Wikimedia Commons; photo: Accurimbono.

CHAPTER 2

Scrolls That Grow

e are particularly aware of the act of enrolling—that is, of entering one's name in the rolls. Similarly, the teacher may call the roll, and the drill sergeant may organize a roll call. Any sort of list or record that is progressive, that is added to from time to time, and that grows over time, is a likely candidate for preservation on a scroll. Scrolls have long been used for record keeping, for financial, legal, and other documents.

Keeping Records: Legal and Financial Documents

A fascinating version of the scroll is not medieval at all, but gives a very good idea of the concept of adding names to a list, of enrolling people. New York State has a series of rolls of attorneys, including one for the Court of Chancery and another for the Supreme Court of Judicature (the latter was the court that produced the longest roll in the state archives).

The tops of many of these scrolls include an oath of office and, early in the new Republic, a citizenship oath; after follows a series of attorneys' dated signatures. These are essentially lists

---

FIG. 2.1

(*Opposite*) The opening image of a version of a Ripley Scroll, an alchemical scroll associated with the name of George Ripley, English alchemist of the fifteenth century. Wellcome Library, London MS 693.

of lawyers in the order they were admitted to the bar. The oaths change with changing times, of course, and that is one reason for starting a new scroll. A law of 1788 required lawyers to sign two oaths: one renouncing allegiance to any foreign king, prince, or potentate and swearing allegiance to the State of New York; and the other swearing to execute their office to the best of their ability. A law of 1796 added an oath to uphold the United States Constitution and a law of 1816 added an antiduelling oath to those already taken by lawyers. The State Constitution of 1821 replaced all previous oaths with one that swore to uphold the state and federal constitutions and to execute one's office to the best of one's ability.

Some of these scrolls are small, consisting of a single sheet of parchment. Others are many yards long and consist of scores of sheets stitched together. The longest roll is some twenty-five feet in length. Like most of the others, it is a series of parchments stitched together with thread (though parchment thongs were sometimes used for this purpose). But it is not one continuous roll, because some of the earlier parchment sheets stitched onto the roll are stitched only at their top edges, so they become flaps within the roll. This roll begins in 1754 and ends in 1847, which is the year that the Supreme Court of Judicature was replaced, on July 1, by a new Supreme Court with offices in each county of the state. This is the only roll with a handle, and a decorative one at that.

Within this roll are several famous names in U.S. history. Of particular note are Aaron Burr and Alexander Hamilton, who were fellow lawyers on the scroll and later were respectively vice-president and secretary of the treasury. The antiduelling oath was added only after the duel in 1804 that resulted in Hamilton's death.

In medieval England, many official records, mostly legal and financial, were kept on scrolls. These were of two types, according to how they were assembled: we might call them Exchequer (financial) scrolls and Chancery (legal) scrolls, after the government departments that used them. Legal matters included everything from royal decrees down to the proceedings of manor courts, the most local unit of the judiciary system. Financial records include those of the Crown, and many local lists of debts, taxes,

FIG. 2.2A

A roll of lawyers of the State of New York, beginning in 1754 and concluding in 1847. Photo Hiroko Masuike/The New York Times/ Redux.

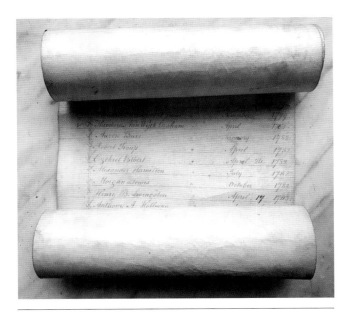

FIG. 2.2B

New York State Supreme Court of Judicature Roll of Attorneys, 1754–1795: One roll consisting of many sheets stitched together. This is a transcription of the original, which must have worn out from use. Pictured are the names of Aaron Burr and Alexander Hamilton, enrolled as attorneys in the same year, with only two others between them. The original would have carried their signatures. Photo: Geof Huth, New York State Unified Court System.

and the like. Such rolls, being the standard way to record such matters, were once very numerous, and today survive in large numbers.

The pipe rolls, maintained by the Exchequer, were the official financial records of the English Crown, and are characteristic of the Exchequer format. Beginning in the twelfth century, they are the oldest and longest set of financial records in Western culture, and provide an unparalleled wealth of historical information. The annual audit of expenses and payments, usually conducted at Michaelmas (September 29), was recorded on sheets of parchment that were stacked one on another and then fastened at the top; the resulting stack was then rolled so that it looked like a conduit or pipe. This unusual form of roll was in use until 1833.

The various pipe rolls contain details of all kinds, allowing for fine-grained observations not always available from the broad sweep of historical chronicles. For example, the Fine Roll for 1263–64 provides the names of some of those rank-and-file knights who fought at the Battle of Lewes between rebel barons led by Simon de Montfort, Earl of Leices-

FIG. 2.3

Pipe roll of the expenses of the estates of the Bishop of Winchester. Note that several documents are placed on a stack before they are rolled into the shape of a pipe. Winchester, Hampshire Record Office.

ter, and the army of King Henry III. On July 21, the scroll records an extraordinary grant: two Dorset knights, Robert Fitz Payn and William de Goviz, were excused a required payment as co-heirs of the Dorset baron Alfred (IV) of Lincoln "for the praiseworthy service which they rendered to the king, and for the losses they sustained in the king's service at Lewes in the battle there."

The Exchequer style of statute roll found in medieval England is made like a pipe roll: several membranes are laid on top of one another, all attached to the same umbilicus along the top margin of each sheet—a bit like newspapers hanging on sticks in hotel lobbies and French cafés—and read by flipping the pages around the central umbilicus to locate the desired information. Statute rolls are legal documents on which are recorded the legislations and laws of communities or individual lords. These scrolls can either serve as the official institution of statutes or as evidence of a judgment between two parties.

There were many legal scrolls; beginning in the late twelfth century, the official legal records were maintained by the Chancery of England, headed by the chancellor. The Master of the Rolls, who had responsibility for keeping the records of the Chancery court, is today the second most senior judge in the English legal system. Rolls were originally stored in the Rolls Chapel in Chancery Lane, London. The Public Record Office, now part of the National Archives, preserves these documents today (surviving parts of the Rolls Chapel are incorporated into the Maughan Library of King's College, London).

Records were kept of all royal and legal acts, many of them on scrolls. All these took the form that is most common in the Middle Ages—membranes were added end to end as the list grew longer, and they were stored in long rolls. There are various types according to their contents: Patent Rolls (kept in this form from 1201 to 2007) record copies of "letters patent," that is, an open letter from the Crown with decrees for all to see. "Letters close," decrees sealed with the royal Great Seal, gave instructions to specific officeholders; these were "enrolled" on Close Rolls (1204–1903). Royal charters, also issued under the Great Seal, comprise the Charter Rolls (1199–1517). Fine Rolls record financial "offerings" to the Crown, beginning with the reign (1199–1216) of King John.

At a local level, many records were kept on scrolls in the Middle Ages. From about the twelfth century, English manors held courts presided over by the lord of the manor. There legal cases were decided and the outcomes recorded on scrolls. Many of these were assembled in Exchequer fashion—that is, by rolling a stack of several sheets fastened together at the top. These records provide a valuable view of rural life in the Middle Ages, and of the lowest rung of a well-ordered legal system.

FIG. 2.4
A Fine Roll from the reign of Henry III of England, being inspected by students in the National Archives. The National Archives, Kew.

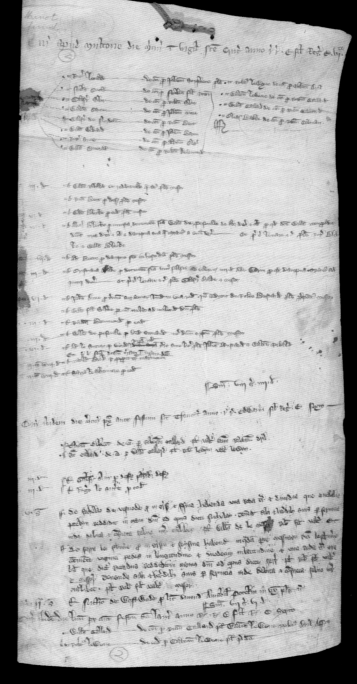

FIG. 2.5

A manor court roll from Cheshire Moulton, England, 1318. This is the top sheet of several that were laced one on top of another and then rolled around a central baton. The text at the top labels the sheet: "Curia apud Multone die Mercurii in vigilem sanctae crucis anno regno regis Edwardi filii regis Edwardi vi" (Court held at Moulton the Wednesday in the Vigil of the Holy Cross, in the regnal year of Edward son of king Edward [i.e. Edward II] 6). The Feast of the Holy Cross was observed on September 14, 1318 (nearing the end of Edward III's sixth year), so the vigil was the Wednesday before, the 13th. Harvard Law School Library, English Manor Rolls, Folder 2.

Gift Lists

The custom of giving and receiving gifts has a long history. Many of us make lists of gifts we intend to give—or at least of persons we propose to give presents to. (A picture of Santa Claus with an enormous scroll listing children and their gifts is a common image in America at Christmastime.) In Elizabethan England gift giving became a carefully regulated and ceremonial affair, and a record was kept of all the gifts presented at the New Year to the monarch, as well as of all the gifts given by the monarch in return. This was the big annual moment of gift giving, far outstripping Christmas and birthdays. The exchanges are essentially between the queen and the ranking nobility who hold offices at court; the more important the office, the more costly the gift to the sovereign, and the more valuable her gift to the noble.

The lists of the gifts, all of them on scrolls, are fascinating documents; twenty-four of them survive from the reign of Elizabeth I, and at least one from her father, Henry VIII. From Henry VIII's gift roll, for example, we know that his preference was for gold. Elizabeth, in contrast, inclined toward clothing, personalized jewelry, and trinkets.

An elaborate ceremony regulated the presentation of gifts at the New Year. A special chamber, prepared in whatever palace the queen found herself, provided long tables for the display of the gifts and for the provision of refreshments. The servants of each of the aristocrats, bishops, and courtiers presented their gifts on behalf of their master or mistress, and received rewards for their trouble. The Lord Chamberlain (the official in charge of court ritual) presided over receipt of the gifts. Each servant then proceeded to the Jewel House, a tower (still standing today) near Westminster Abbey, where each was assigned to return home with the queen's gift in return, determined by the rank of the recipient and the value of the gift received.

Among the gifts presented to the queen were purses made of precious materials and filled with coins or clothing, gloves, jewelry, musical instruments. There were various custodians and repositories, depending on the type of gift, and the record indicates which official takes charge of each gift, usually according to category.

Each scroll has a list of gifts to the queen at the front, with her signature at the top. The surviving rolls name more than 1,200 people, of whom about a third are women. The donors are listed in order of their standing: blood relatives of the queen; dukes, marquesses, and earls; bishops; duchesses and countesses; viscounts; lords; ladies, knights, chaplains, gentlewomen, gentlemen. The back side lists the gifts of the queen to her courtiers, in essentially the same descending order of precedence.

In 1559, George Rotheridge gave the Queen a two-year-old lion; there is a blank in the scroll where normally is written an indication of who is to take charge of the gift. One imagines everybody's reluctance to take custody of this gift . . .

Here is an excerpt from the list of 1588–89:

Newe Yeare's Guiftes gyven to the Queene's Majesty at Her Highnes Mannour of Richmond, by these Parsons whose names do hereafter ensewe, the first daye, the yeare aforesaide.

. . . . [here we skip certain high officials, earls and viscounts]

Marquesse and Countesses.

By the Lady Marquesse of *Northampton*, a peire of braceletts of gold conteyning 16 peeces, four enamuled white set with one pearle in a peece, and four sparks of rubyes a peece, the other foure sett with one dasy and a small ruby in the middest thereof, and four small pearles and eight longe peeces betwene them, ech sett with small diamonds and two sparks of rubyes.

Delivered to the said Mrs. *Ratcliff*.

By the Countesse of *Shrewsbury*, a safegard with a jhup or gaskyn coat of faire cullored satten, like flames of fire of gold, and garnesshed with buttons, loupes, and lace of Venis silver.

Delivered to the Roabes.

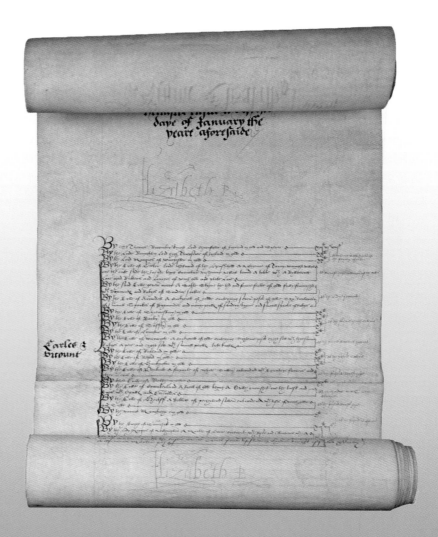

FIG. 2.6

The New Year's Gift Roll for Queen Elizabeth I created in 1585. The queen has
signed the roll at top and bottom, on both sides. In addition to listing on the front
the gifts presented to her, the reverse of the roll records her gifts in return (always
in the rather unimaginative, if valuable, form of gilt plate). Presents given to the
queen vary considerably: one of the presents listed here is a grand gown from Sir
Francis Walsingham: "A French goune of Russett Satten Floryshed with Leves of
Sylver bound Aboute with a passamayne of venis golde with pendante sleves Lyned
with Cloth of Sylver."

This is one of six gift rolls held by the Folger Shakespeare Library; this example
is written on 11½ feet of vellum. Washington, The Folger Shakespeare Library MS
Z.d.16.

By the Countesse of *Huntington*, in gold, 8 s
> Delivered to the said Mr. *Sackford*.

By the Countesse of *Warwick*, a chayne, containing 22 aggetts slytely garnesshed with gold, and 22 bawles of jheat slytely garnesshed over with seede pearles.
> Delivered to the said Mrs. *Ratcliff*.

By the Countesse of *Lyncoln*, widdowe, a longe cloake of murry velvet, with a border rounde aboute of a small chenye lace of Venis silver, and two rowes of buttons and lowpes of like silver furred thorough with mynnyover and calloper like myll pykes.
> Delivered to the Roabes.

The gifts from the queen were entirely objects of silver gilt—bowls, stoups, and cups, usually with a cover—all carefully weighed. The gilt pieces were ordered from a group of London silversmiths and kept in the Jewel House until they were called for by the servants of the recipients. The Master of the Jewel House was in charge of keeping the gifts in order, and for drafting the lists that made up the scrolls.

Mortuary Rolls: Scrolls on the Road

On September 16, 1122, the beloved and esteemed founding abbot of the monastery of Savigny in Normandy died at the age of sixty-two. Vitalis was a much-admired churchman, later a hermit, and finally the founder of the monastery of Savigny, where he gained a great reputation as a preacher. Born at Mortain near Bayeux, he became chaplain to Robert, brother of William the Conqueror, and was appointed to a plush canonry at Mortain. But he longed for a purer religious life and retired to lead a colony of hermits in the forest, where his ministry and preaching attracted a group of people around him. This congregation became the monastery of the Holy Trinity at Savigny, with Vitalis at its head. It ultimately grew into the Congregation of Savigny, grouping together a large number of monasteries and convents in France and England: ironic, perhaps, that a hermit seeking isolation ends his life at the head of a large organization.

The founder's death was an important event. Vitalis's community chose to spread the sad news in the customary way for such significant moments. An official announcement of the death was written on a scroll, which was then carried by a roll bearer (*rolliger*, or *rotulifer*) designated by the monastery to neighboring and related monasteries. Each of these then added their prayers for the repose of Vitalis's soul. Often they added poems or other uplifting texts, or requests for reciprocal prayers. This mortuary roll, as these traveling announcements are often called, traveled to neighboring convents, to other monasteries of the same order, and to many churches. As the roll traveled, it grew longer, since each place on the itinerary added its own prayers for Vitalis and its own request that others pray for them. Vitalis's scroll was taken to 207 monasteries in Normandy and England during 1123 and 1124, and grew to be over thirty feet long. (We can't be sure of the exact length because the beginning of the scroll is now missing.)

The roll bearer (who sometimes had the roll attached around his neck so that it could not be removed) was expected to be treated with courtesy, received with hospitality, and, in some monasteries at least, provided with a financial reward.

Mortuary scrolls dating from the ninth century until well into the fifteenth are one of the most interesting and informative medieval phenomena for those interested in handwriting, travel, and many other things. When, as often happened, the date of the roll's arrival at each of its stops is given, we can trace the itinerary of the scroll and learn exactly how long it took to go from place A to place B. (The rolls are also a good antidote to the idea that handwriting can be dated and localized; in a given region at a specific time there can be an enormous variety of hands and styles of writing.)

When Vitalis's mortuary scroll passed by the convent of Argenteuil in 1123, it may well have been Héloise who composed the beautiful elegy on Vitalis's death that is inscribed on the scroll. Héloise, unusually for a woman of her time, was a famous scholar, the wife of the philosopher Peter Abelard. For now, she was living among the nuns at Argenteuil, where she had been brought up. Héloise later became head of the convent of the Paraclete, where Peter Abelard later became abbot and provided many hymns and other materials for the nuns. Together, Abelard and Héloise edited a collection of their love letters and other correspondence that we still read today.

Meanwhile, the scroll traveled on, crossing the English Channel to make the rounds of monasteries and cathedrals in southern England before returning to the monastery treasury at Savigny. The scroll is now held in the Musée des Archives Nationales in Paris.

There were many other mortuary scrolls like that of Vitalis. Travel time was variable: a roll could remain for weeks at a single church or monastery. Sometimes the delivery was urgent and travel time swift. The rotulifer who announced the death of Jean II de Marigny, abbot of St. Étienne in Dijon, was one of the quickest on record. Between April 1401 and March 1402, he visited 516 churches. The speed and distance indicates that this messenger (whose name was Denis) wasted no time. On July 22, 1401, he managed to collect *tituli* at Castelnaudary and at Toulouse, thirty-four miles distant, having stopped on the way at Mas-St. Puelles. And setting out on August 1, 1401, it took him only two days to cover the 124 miles between Rodez and Le Puy. He must have had a fast horse.

Cooking, Medicine, and Alchemy

Cooking, medicine, and alchemy have a lot in common: they all require lists of recipes, ingredients, and procedures for producing the desired result. And a scroll is a good place for such lists, partly because it can grow, and partly because it can be opened to the recipe wanted. Many modern cooks might find such an arrangement useful; indeed, those who consult recipes on their tablets are doing just that.

One of the grandest of medieval cookbooks was made for King Richard II of England (1367–1400). He had a series of expert cooks who compiled a list of recipes that survives in two scrolls (one in New York and one in London); a third copy is in codex form. All three contain versions of a text dating from the fourteenth century known as *The*

The mortuary roll of Vitalis, abbot of Savigny, who died on September 16, 1122. The image shows a portion of the scroll sent to announce his death. Made of successive sheets held together by strips of parchment threaded through slits (visible here at top and bottom), the roll measures 32 feet × 8–9 inches wide. The beginning of it is now missing, but the whole text survives in a later copy. In the portion shown here, the scroll has arrived in England. The red "T" at the top marks the first of three stops in Winchester ("Titulus sancti Petri et sancti Swithuni Wintoniensis"); then Rumsey Abbey in Hampshire (the second black "T": "Titulus Sancte Marie Rumesiensis ecclesie"), where prayers are asked for the prioress Petronilla, for the precentor Cecilia, and for the sisters Godiva, Visla, Leoviva, Beata, Gilburga, and all the deceased nuns of the abbey. The roll then records travels to Salisbury Cathedral ("Titulus Sancte Marie Salesburiensis"), where a poem in honor of Vitalis is added, and to Shaftesbury Abbey (the title written in green and orange), and on to Milton and beyond. Archives nationales, France.

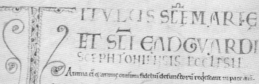

FIG. 2.7B

A map showing the itinerary of the mortuary roll of Vitalis of Savigny in 1123–24. Starting at Savigny it zigzags around ecclesiastical France as far south as Chateauroux, as far north as Laon, with dense travels through Normandy. Passing through Savigny again, it crosses the English Channel and arrives at Bosham, where it begins an extensive tour of English cathedrals and convents. © OpenStreetMap Contributors, Carto, and Aaron Macks.

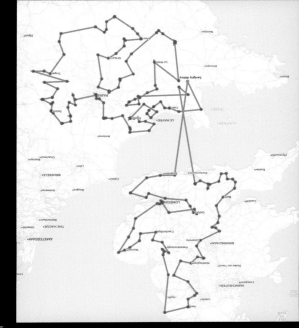

FIG. 2.7C

The beginning of the inscription of the titulus of the convent church at Argenteuil, where Héloise was prioress:

> The title of the convent church of Saint Mary in Argenteuil.
>
> May the soul of Vitalis, and the souls of all the faithful departed, rest in the true peace which is Christ. We have prayed for yours; pray for us and for ours: count Baldwin; abbesses Basilia, Adele, Judith; the nuns Helvide and Adele; the dean Eremburga; Adelaide and Havida, Dodone the layman, and all whose names the Lord may write in the book of life. Amen.

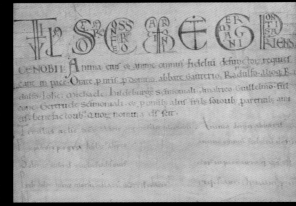

Then follows a poem that some scholars attributed to Héloise; it is an inspired and noble elegy that begins as follows, with my translation:

> Flet pastore pio grex desolatus adempto
> Soletur miseras turba fidelis oves.
> Proh dolor! hunc morsu sublatum mortis edaci
> Non dolor aut gemitus vivificare queunt.

The desolate flock mourns its faithful shepherd now taken away
The faithful multitude must comfort the poor sheep,
Oh sadness! him whom Death snatches with his devouring sting,
Neither sadness nor wailing can bring him back to life.

Forme of Cury, or "the (proper) method of cookery." It is by far the best-known guide to medieval cooking. The preamble to the text explains that the work has been given the "assent and avysement of Maisters and phisik and of philosophie that dwelled in his court" (the assent and advice of the masters of medicine and of philosophy). The close relationship of cuisine, medicine, and science was evidently already well known at that time.

The list of recipes furnishes a remarkable look at culinary practices in the fourteenth century. There are some two hundred recipes for dishes ranging from the very simple "common pottages and common meats for the household, as they should be made, craftily and wholesomely" to the complex, ornate, and spicy dishes for banquets, "curious potages and meetes and sotiltees [subtleties] for alle maner of States bothe hye and lowe."

The recipes in these lists are not arranged like those in most modern cookbooks—appetizers, soups, main courses, etc.—but in a sort of accretive order, suggesting a collection that grows longer over time. Neither of the surviving scrolls, however, gives evidence of being added to in this way; they are intended, it seems, to be complete, so the scroll form may be meant mainly to be accessible and portable.

Spices, colors, scents, appearance—all were important in the presentation of dishes recommended in the list. Many animals were served that are no longer in vogue: one recipe reads, in its entirety, "Cranys and Herons schulle be euarud [adorned?] wyth Lardons of swine and rostyd and etyn with gyngenyr."

A great—albeit expensive and luxurious—range of spices is called for: saffron, cardamom, cinnamon, mace, cloves, ginger, galyngal (a relative of ginger), pepper, cubeb (Java pepper), nutmeg, and caraway. There is much honey, and also sugar, which was beginning to become common. There is not much butter; instead, there is lard (often called "grese"or "grees"), and a very early reference in English to olive oil. Wine is mentioned, both local and imported from France, the Rhineland, and Greece.

Standard seasoning mixtures had French names like powder-fort and powder-douce. The former is a pulverized mixture of strong spices:

pepper, ginger, and others. Powder-douce is a gentler and sweeter mixture; both are kept at the ready for frequent use.

Many recipes seem to require grinding, pulverizing, and generally avoiding large pieces of food that might require a fork. One such recipe is for mawmenny:

FOR TO MAKE MAWMENNY
Take the chese and of flessh of capouns, or of hennes & hakke smal and grynde hem smale inn a morter, take mylke of almandes with the broth of freysh beef, other freysh flessh, & put the flessh in the mylke over in the broth and set hem to the fyre, & alye hem with flour of ryse, or gastbon, or amydoun as chargeaunt as the blank desire, & with zolks of ayren and safroun for to make hit zelow, and when it is dressit in dysshes with blank desires; styk aboue clowes de gilofre, & strawe powdour of galyugale above, and serue it forth.

My interpretation in modern language:

Take cheese and flesh of capons, or of hens, and hack small and grind them small in a mortar; take milk of almonds with the broth of fresh beef, other fresh flesh, and put the flesh in the milk in the broth and set them to the fire, and thicken it with rice flour, or the finest bread (cf. Fr. *gateau*), or amydoun (fine wheat flour steeped in water, strained, dried in the sun), as stiff as the blanc desire (a white dish of crushed fowl-meat, almond milk, and spices), and with yolks of eggs and saffron to make it yellow, and when it is dressed in dishes and blanc desire, stick above it cloves, and strew it with powder of galyngale (a form of ginger), and serve it forth.

Some of the recipes in the scrolls are for fairly simple dishes; but others are highly complex ones suitable for the royal table. Exactly what King Richard II enjoyed at his meals is more than these scrolls tell us, but we can see perhaps one extreme of royal dining in the banquet given in honor of King Richard by John Fordham, the Bishop of Durham, at his palace in London in 1387. A description of the menu survives in a fifteenth-century cookbook. (Again, some of the spellings below have been modernized for clarity.) The banquet is in three courses, each course consisting of many dishes placed on the table all together. It is up to the diner to help himself to whatever is near at hand, and it is unlikely that everybody has some of each item, especially since a lot of roast meats and game are repeated at each course.

Each course is marked by a "Sotelte." Such "subtleties" were elaborate sculptural presentations, made of pastry, sugar, and other ingredients, which served to mark the boundaries of the courses. They were very large, and might represent animals, buildings, allegorical or mythological figures, or fully rigged ships. Some famous subtleties included musicians inside, or singing birds (as in "four and twenty blackbirds baked in a pie").

This is the purviaunce made for Kinge Richard, beings with The Duke of Lancastre at the Bisshoppes place of Durham at London, the 23d day of September, the year of the kinge aforsaid the twelft [1387]

THE FIRST COURSE.
Venison with Furmenty (a sweet porridge of wheat).
A potage called viaundbruse (meat stew).
Hedes of Boars.
Great Flessh (joints of meat?).
Swannes rosted.
Pigges rosted.
Custarde lumbard in paste (custard of wine, dates, and honey in pastry).
And a Sotelte.

THE SECONDE COURSE.
A potage called Gele (gelée, jelly?)
A potage de Blandesore (see blank desire above!).
Pigges roasted.

Cranes roasted.

Pheasants roasted.

Herons roasted. Chekens endored (gilded with egg yolk).

Breame.

Tartes.

Broken brawn (jellied meat).

Coneys (rabbits) roasted.

And a sotellte.

THE THIRDE COURSE.

Potage bruete of Almondes (almonds, honey, eggs).

Stewed lumbarde (honey, dates, wine).

Venyson roasted.

Chekenes roasted.

Rabettes roasted.

Partridge rosted.

Pigeons roasted.

Quailes roasted.

Larkes roasted.

Payne puff (little loaves of bread)

A Dish of Gely.

Longe Fritters.

And a Sotelte.

It is easy to imagine that such a feast was not an everyday occurrence. The bishop was entertaining the king, and doing so in royal style. One imagines that on other days, the bishop and the king likely ate somewhat more simply.

Medicine and Magic

An early example of mixture of pharmacy, medicine, and the practice of incantations is a scroll of the end of the eleventh century, some twenty feet long, written on both sides, and full of interesting information about

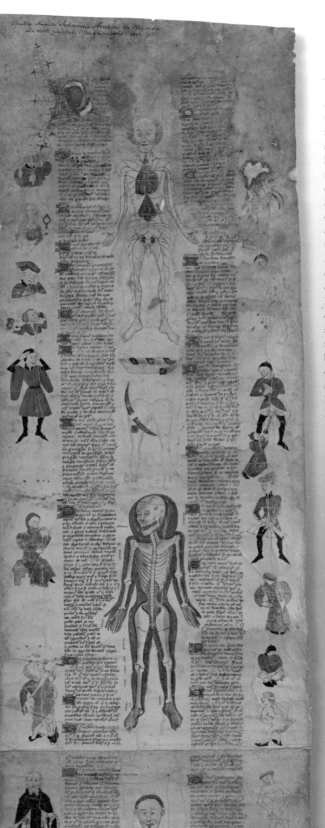

FIG. 2.8

A scroll of medical and surgical treatises largely by the great fourteenth-century English surgeon John Arderne. It may have been prepared about 1430 for Princess Phillippa, wife of Eric, King of Denmark, Sweden, and Norway. The title of Arderne's treatise on medicine and surgery appears at the top of the left column in brown and red: *Practica Magistri Johannis Ardeni de Newarti (Newark-on-Trent) de arte physicali et de Cirurgia.* In the center are drawings of the circulatory system and of the skeleton; along the left side are illustrations of various maladies: baldness, sleeplessness, headache, etc. Rather less pleasant maladies and treatments are on the right. National Library of Sweden MS X 118.

medicine and magic. Originating perhaps in the Alsatian monastery of Murbach, it includes a Latin-German glossary of plant names.

But the main content of the scroll—the whole front side and the first half of the back—consists of numerous incantations and blessings, some medical treatises about paralysis, and a great deal more. There are recipes, generally for medicaments, including how to cure back pain, to chase away snakes, to alleviate kidney stones, to treat various kinds of pain, and to ward off bad dogs, baldness, and the "Teutonic paralysis" (*Contra paralysin theutonice*). There are some pretty gruesome—by our standards—formulas to stop bleeding, most of them more religious, or magical, than medical. Here's an example.

+ [make the sign of the cross] Christ went to the Jordan, to be baptized by John. The Jordan stood and was stilled (this refers to an apocryphal story). Likewise let these drops of blood be stilled, which fall from the nostrils of this man *Name*. Let the blood stop. I adjure you [a formula used in exorcisms] by the name of Christ: let the blood stop. +Let the blood stop. + Let the blood stop.

Another fascinating medical scroll may have been made for the Queen of Sweden. In 1406, the twelve-year-old English princess Phillippa, daughter of King Henry IV of England (who deposed Richard II, he of the huge banquet), married Eric, king of Norway, Sweden, and Denmark. Her grandfather's physician, John Arderne (1307–1392), was a pioneer in surgery, and it is probably no accident that Arderne's medical treatises are preserved in a scroll found in Sweden. It is nice to think that the scroll might have been prepared for a princess in a distant land.

The scroll, written and illustrated in London about 1430 (when Phillippa was thirty-six) is some six yards long and seven inches wide. It includes two treatises by Arderne: a general manual on medicine and surgery (*De arte physicali et de chirurgia*), including an influential article on rectal disorders, and a treatise on obstetrics.

Arderne is considered by many to be the father of surgery. He saw military service in the Hundred Years' War, and witnessed some of the first effects of gunpowder at the siege of Algeciras (1342–44). Arderne is remembered for the works he wrote, in Latin, towards the end of his life, recommending treatments for various ailments and case histories. He was trained, as most surgeons were, by apprenticeship and learning on the job. His practical experience led to useful observations and techniques, some of which are still in use. But he was a physician of his time, and counted on bloodletting and on astrology as important parts of medicine, since it was believed that each sign of the zodiac affects a different part of the body.

Not all his recommendations are practiced today, of course. For example: "In every affection of the heart, of epilepsy and future leprosy. R. Decoction of the bone of a stag's heart given in wine with powdered pearls. If juice of borage be added it will be more effective."

Arderne's works are found in other sources; this scroll form may be unique. Was it actually used as a reference during surgical treatment, kept open to the relevant portion, or was the scroll format chosen for portability or to lend the contents some sort of authenticity?

Alchemy and Magic

Several surviving medieval scrolls combine magic and medicine with alchemy. They contain magical spells of all kinds, such as how to incite fierceness; what charms work for love or for fishing; how to calm down fire; and even how to make a horse lame. These are combined with technical and medicinal recipes and lengthy alchemical processes. Such scrolls seem to be compendia of practical knowledge, mixing areas of expertise that we now consider separately.

It is not surprising that medical and alchemical information was collected in a single document: in the medieval view, they were branches of a universal science. Alchemy, brought to Europe through translations of Arabic treatises, focuses on the essences of physical materials; as such, it was a sort of science, and was in many ways the precursor of chemistry. Like astrology, its sister science, alchemy seeks to relate the physical and visible world to the greater universe of the unseen. Effects achieved and observed in the physical world bear a relationship to the human being, so that transmutations of elements can correspond to transmutations of the spirit. These correspondences and processes are at the heart of the alchemical process. Symbols, colors, and codes make alchemical texts a sort of secret language, which only people who were adept at this craft could fully understand. The scrolls show how magic (which deals with supernatural powers), alchemy (physical processes), and astrology (celestial bodies and motions) all were seen in the relation of their subject matter to human beings, and were brought to bear on lives, relationships, and actions.

Among the most notable alchemical scrolls are twenty-three documents associated with George Ripley, one of England's most famous alchemists. These scrolls are large and magnificently illustrated demonstrations of alchemical principles. They are surely not designed for portability—no alchemist would lay one on his table to follow a recipe. They are display scrolls, probably only created in scroll format as a sign of their importance.

Ripley, born about 1415, was a canon regular—a sort of monk— in the Augustinian priory of Bridlington in Yorkshire. (Although the Ripley Scrolls bear his name, he may actually have very little to do with them.) He traveled to France, Germany, and Italy in search of alchemical knowledge and to the island of Rhodes, where he was a patron of the Knights of St. John of Jerusalem (now known as the Knights of Malta). He returned to England in 1471 and wrote many alchemical works, the most famous being the *Compound of Alchymy, or, the Twelve Gates leading to the Discovery of the Philosopher's Stone.*

The scrolls themselves all seem to descend from a fifteenth-century original. Even though some of them contain verses associated with Ripley, there is no evidence that the alchemist himself made the original design. A Ripley scroll is essentially a series of highly detailed pictures, with substantial commentary.

The opening picture in the scroll reproduced on page 40 is of the alchemist himself, or perhaps the idealized alchemist. Some say it represents Aristotle, or even Hermes Trismegistus (the legendary author of

FIG. 2.9A

A Ripley scroll, sixteenth century. Below the alchemist is a "Philosophical Tree" growing from a fountain in which cavort nude male and female figures and around which stand other, clothed, figures bearing beakers. On the tree are figures, including a remarkable frog-woman with a serpent's tail. The fountain is supported on a column, borne by the figure of Terra, the earth, rising from a square pool of yellow fluid, with four towers representing the four elements; curious figures, one winged "Spiritus—water") and one ringed with fire ("Anima—oyle"), stand ankle-deep in the pool. Below them a green dragon spews out a fire-breathing toad ("The tuyning Venome"); beneath them, "Heare is the somme the whiche is called the mouth of the Colloricke [choleric?]." then red and yellow lions flanking a fire labeled "collorick," labeled "The mouthe of the Collorick beware."

FIG. 2.9B

Continuation of the Ripley scroll
at the Wellcome Library, London,
MS 693, sixteenth century: "Hear
is the laste of the read Stone and
the beginninge to put away the
dead the Elixir vitae" floats over
a blazing sun, under which a
golden bird, with the head of a
bearded and crowned old man,
stands on a black globe studded
with feathers, all surrounded by a
rain of golden drops. Underneath,
a verse is followed by "The Birde
of Hermes is my name: eating
my winges: to make me tame."
Next comes a pointy sunburst,
in gold and black, with three
linked colored stones (labeled
"The white Stone; The Red
Stone; The Elixir vitae"), above
a tricolor crescent moon held by
a dragon bleeding onto a winged
orb divided into three. A panel of
verse is followed by a man holding
a staff with a pen, with a roll of
parchment or paper wrapped
around it at one end and a horse's
hoof at the other end. This figure
concludes one of the five sections
of this remarkable scroll.

the sacred texts of hermeticism). A ribbon-like scroll over his head says, "Est lapis Occultus secreto fonte Sepultus" (This is the hidden stone, buried in the secret fountain).

The alchemist lightly touches an alchemical "egg," or hermetic vessel, which is placed on a plate over a flame. Inside, a toad appears above a series of eight linked roundels. Seven of them, each illustrating one of seven alchemical processes, are linked to a central image of two figures, a monk and a king, holding a closed book; these are the seven seals of the Book of Revelation, containing wisdom acquired through the alchemical processes.

The handles of the vessel direct: "You muste make water of the Earth and earth of the Ayre and Aire of the fier and fier of the Earth." As all alchemists believed at the time, each of the four elements was a manifestation of the *prima materia*, and could be converted into the others. This principle also allowed the transmutation of one metal into another.

The black toad, surrounded by drops of blood and falling feathers, symbolizes all that is dark: earth, blackness, overeating, poisonousness, death. An alchemist who called himself Eirenaeus Philalethes ("Peaceful lover of truth") composed a "Vision of Sir George Ripley," which includes the following lines:

> *When busie at my Book I was upon a certain Night,*
> *This Vision here exprest appear'd unto my dimmed sight:*
> *A Toad full Ruddy I saw, did drink the juice of Grapes so fast,*
> *Till over-charged with the broth, his Bowels all to-brast.*

The seven stages in the alchemical process involve working on the *prima materia* depicted in the first roundel (the one not linked to the book). This shows man and woman linked to sun and moon, with various animals, some of which were labeled, in Latin, "green lion" and "red lion."

The plate on which the beaker sits reads: "Heare is the laste of the white Stoane: And the begininge of the read Stoane." Flanking the sides of the red dot at the bottom of the beaker are: "The blacke Sea: The blacke Lune: The blacke Sol." The color imagery continues throughout the scroll, and is central to the alchemical process. The move from the white stone (the agent for the transmutation of base metals) to the beginning of the red (that which produces gold) has begun.

It is amazing how much information is provided, albeit in cryptic form, in each of the images in the Ripley scrolls.

Armorial Rolls

Some scrolls are collections of aristocratic coats of arms, especially in England, where social standing has always been of high importance. Most surviving armorial scrolls, and a great many copies of them (and of other kinds of scrolls) are English in origin. Arms are originally the decorations painted on shields to allow knights to be recognized in tournaments—rather like the silks that modern-day racing jockeys wear. Heralds needed to be able to announce the identity of riders hidden by their suits of armor, and the discipline of heraldry has its origin with the heralds on the field of combat, whether ceremonial or not.

The term survives today in announcements, such as "Hark the herald angels . . ." and newspapers such as *The Blattburg Daily Herald*, or it can designate officials who survey and control armorial bearings: the science of armorial bearings is *heraldry*.

The earliest surviving armorial roll is the Dering Roll, made in Dover about 1270–1280. It pictures the coats of arms of 324 knights, starting with two illegitimate children of King John. It is named for its seventeenth-century owner, Sir Edward Dering (1598–1644), antiquary and lieutenant of Dover Castle in Kent, who probably altered the names above a few shields to provide himself with some titled ancestors.

The shields are arranged in rows of six across, descending through fifty-four rows in six vertical membranes.

Armorial rolls from France, the Netherlands, Germany, and Italy have also been preserved. Coats of arms are also collected in other forms, of course, including codices; the use of scrolls for this purpose might be explained as providing for future expansion, although most surviving documents give limited evidence of this.

FIG. 2.10A
The Dering Roll, the earliest
English armorial scroll, made
about 1270–1280, comprises
four pieces of parchment,
with 324 shields arranged in
fifty-four rows of six each. The
shields are painted on a green
background. The arms are
predominantly those of knights
of Kent and Sussex, and include
fifteen sheriffs of Kent and four
constables of Dover Castle,
a list of the knights owing
feudal service to the Constable
of Dover Castle. It may have
been commissioned by Stephen
of Penchester, who served as
Constable from 1268 to 1298.

This roll is now in the British
Library in London. It once
belonged to Sir Anthony Wagner,
who had the wonderful title of
Garter Principal King of Arms at
the Royal College of Arms, and
whose catalog of English armorial
sources is indispensable. In 2007,
the roll was sold at Sotheby's for
£192,000. The purchaser sought
to export it, but the culture
ministry was able to delay the
export, and the British Library,
with the help of many donors,
enlisted enough support to add
the roll to its collection, where it
is now displayed.

A detailed and fascinating
discussion of the roll is provided
by the British Library at http://
britishlibrary.typepad.co.uk/
digitisedmanuscripts/2014/10/
heraldic-herrings-hedgehogs-and-
hosiery.html#. British Library,
MS Additional Roll 77720, f. 4v.

FIG. 2.10B

Detail from the Dering Roll. The British Library's commentary points out the designs for Nicholas le Lou (Old French *leu*, *lou*, wolf), Henry de Herice (Old French *hérisson*, hedgehog), Nicholas de la Heuse (Old French *hose*, *huese*, *heuse*, men's hose), and Henry de Cockington, appropriately represented by two wolves, three hedgehogs, three stockings, and nine cocks, respectively. In the arcane language of heraldry, the descriptions of the arms in the top two rows read as follows (a few color words: gules = red, argent = silver, sable = black, or = gold):

> *Willem de Prestone: Gules crusily and a bend or*
> *Robert Eneby: Paly argent and gules, a bend sable*
> *Robert la Warde: Vair argent and sable*
> *Nicole le Leu: Gules, two wolves passant argent*
> *Henri de Herice: Or, three hedgehogs statant sable*
> *Walter FizHonfrey: Quarterly argent and sable*
> *Nicole de la Heuse: Argent, three stockings gules*
> *Richard de Welles: Gules, two pales or, on a canton argent a mullet sable*
> *Henri de Perk: Argent, a stag's head gules*
> *Willem Mansel: Gules, a fess argent, a label or*
> *Jon de Stavertone: Argent fretty gules*
> *Herbert de Seint Quintin: Or, three chevrons gules, a chief vair*

In many cases it is hard to know whether the original document was a scroll. Scholars and practitioners of heraldry (those people with titles like "Garter King of Arms") often refer to a "roll of arms," when what they mean is a roster or a list that could be preserved in scroll form or not. Many such surviving "rolls" are copies, now in the form of a codex, of an earlier "roll of arms" whose original form cannot be determined. Thus, we cannot be sure of the sources in all cases.

Another particularly interesting armorial roll dates from about 1340 and includes color illustrations of the arms of noble families of Swabia, including the area around Lake Constance, German-speaking Switzerland, and Alsace. Its four strips, five inches high, originally totaled thirteen feet in horizontal length. One of the strips has been lost, but its contents survive in two copies. The original now has a total

of 559 coats of arms and twenty-eight banners of bishops; 108 were on the lost portion.

The Zurich scroll is unusual in its manufacture. Most armorial scrolls are painted in successive rows of emblems starting at the top (like the Dering Roll), with the number of emblems in each row depending on the width of the scroll. The Zurich scroll, however, is oriented horizontally, with two rows of emblems, one above the other. The back side is painted, too, in the opposite direction, with the first emblem on the top row back placed behind the last of the top row on the front.

How was the scroll made? Some scholars think that the scribe-illustrator filled out the top row all the way across the front of all four strips of the scroll (presumably sliding the scroll across a desk or table and allowing the ends to curl or droop off the edges), and then began

FIG. 2.11
The beginning of the Zurich heraldic scroll. The scroll is written from left to right, and contains two rows of coats of arms. Zurich, Swiss National Museum DIG-24119.

again with the second row; only then did he turn the scroll over and begin with the top row on the back side.

The shields are not painted in vertical pairs; sometimes there are additional emblems above or below, so it seems likely, especially given the relationships of shields, that emblems were added in groups, using both rows, as the scribe moved across the strip. What is not clear is whether the whole length of the front was used before any of the back was illustrated; and we can't be sure whether the scribe started with the almost six hundred emblems, or whether the available space was filled out until the scroll was full.

Whatever the planning process that produced this scroll, it emphasizes that scrolls have peculiar requirements and peculiar opportunities. Mostly, scribes did not use the back of a scroll. As noted earlier, continuing on the back from the end of the front allows the reader to continue without rewinding the whole scroll but makes it difficult to lengthen the scroll if items need to be added. Alternatively, continuing on the back by starting again at the beginning of the scroll is inconvenient for the user because the scroll must be rewound.

The scrolls discussed in this chapter are similar in that their contents are lists of some kind: records, prayers, recipes, prescriptions, shields. These are all collections that are conducive to getting longer, and some of these documents may have been made in scroll form to make this possible. Many of them, however, are so beautifully made—like the Ripley alchemical scrolls—that it seems equally likely that the purpose of the scrolls was to impress readers with the solemnity that the form implies. The origin of this type of scroll, however, is a list that can be lengthened.

There are many types of list-making scrolls that aren't mentioned at all here. Petitions to the English parliament were often presented on scrolls in the Middle Ages. The University of Paris sent its annual list of requests for appointments and benefices to the Pope on a scroll. Benefices, mostly renewed annually, were what kept the mostly-clergy teaching staff of the university solvent (the scrolls themselves don't survive, but

they can be reconstructed from transcriptions in the Vatican Archives).
The testimony of witnesses in medieval trials was often taken down on
a scroll (rather like the paper scroll issuing from the court reporter's old
stenograph machine). Scrolls listed properties confiscated by the Crown
in England; rent rolls, lists of the possessions of churches, and anything
else whose text comprises a series of short entries, were a good candidate
for scroll format.

Aquy esta a sera dos montes cl ng

meoterano delebante

Grega

yenesia

J. debuda   J. de Janzi   vinegia

uropa parte dalemanha

CHAPTER 3

Representing Space and Time: The Long Red Line

U sing length to represent time or space was a frequent reason for making a scroll. Genealogies and histories of various kinds can be depicted as continuous; for example, a history of the world in biblical terms or a line of descent can be rendered as an unbroken line when you don't have to turn a page. Travel guides, such as how to get to Rome or to the Holy Land, are sometimes laid out in scrolls, where the route can be shown as an uninterrupted line.

Maps and Guides

A map—or at least a certain kind of map—is a perfect candidate for a scroll. Anybody who has tried to refold a complex roadmap knows that a strip that has your point of origin at one end and your destination at the other would be a much better solution. This sort of map works, however, for only one itinerary. But for important itineraries, such as how to get to Rome, to Jerusalem, to Contantinople, such maps can have the advantage of putting

---

DETAIL FIG. 3.1
(*Opposite*) Detail of Portolan, or nautical chart of the Mediterranean area
(*see page 77*).

useful information together in a small space where only the currently needed part of the trip is referenced.

❖ TABULA PEUTINGERIANA

Surely the most famous map in scroll form is a thirteenth-century document that shows itineraries of the late Roman world. It is not a single-trip map; instead, it seeks to put absolutely everything about travel into a single document. It is amazing that it survives for us to see today.

Now called the *Tabula Peutingeriana* (Peutinger's map), it is named for Konrad Peutinger (1465–1547), a distinguished scholar and biblio-

phile, economist, collector, and a town clerk of the city of Augsburg. He also served as adviser to the emperors Maximilian I and Charles V, and he inherited this remarkable scroll from his friend the scholar and imperial librarian Konrad Celtes.

To advise Maximilian and Charles V was heady stuff for a town clerk. Maximilian, by his marriage to Mary of Burgundy, added the extensive duchy of Burgundy to his holdings as Holy Roman Emperor; his grandson Charles V inherited all that from him, and added to it the kingdoms of Castile and Aragon, making the House of Hapsburg rulers of a large portion of Europe.

Peutinger was an important person in his own world. He negoti-

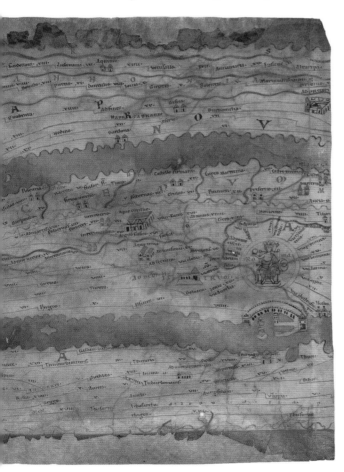

FIG. 3.2
The *Tabula Peutingeriana*. This map, probably a medieval copy of a much older Roman map, is of enormous value to historians. It is named for an early owner, the Renaissance humanist Konrad Peutinger. In this detail, the City of Rome is represented as a crowned emperor enthroned and seated in a circle. From it radiate, in red, the various roads (all of which, as we know, lead to Rome); to the right, the Via Tyburtina (Tiburtina), Via Prenestina, Via Lavicana (Labicana), Via Latina, Via Appia, Via Hostiensis (Ostiensis) lead away to the east and south. To the left of the city, outside the circle is the basilica of Saint Peter on the Vatican hill, labeled in red "SCM PE-TRUM" (Sanctum Petrum). The Port is towards the bottom of the map, and across a very narrow sea from it is northern Africa. Rivers are shown in green (the Tiber flows through the city). Austrian National Library, Vienna, Cod. 324.

ated between the emperors and their bankers, the Fuggers and Welsers of Augsburg. He was a noted humanist, corresponding with the likes of Erasmus of Rotterdam. He published an important series of Roman inscriptions. Peutinger is remembered today, though, mostly for his scroll, which was actually discovered by the distinguished scholar and librarian Konrad Celtes, who turned it over to Peutinger for publication. It was not published in its entirety, however, until 1753.

The scroll is in eleven long strips, each one showing a lengthy slice of the world; when laid side by side they represent vertical slices of "the World" from Britain in the west to India and onward in the east. (A twelfth strip, showing the Iberian peninsula, must be lost.) Each strip reads horizontally, with north on the left and south on the right. Laid out for travelers, the map shows roads, cities, ferries, rivers—things that matter to people planning or making a trip. The map is not to scale; it omits many things that perhaps don't matter and includes others—the city of Pompeii (destroyed in 79 CE) is there, and so is Constantinople (founded in 328). It also juxtaposes things that aren't really adjacent— such as the end points of crossings of rivers and seas.

The *Tabula Peutingeriana* is a skewed version of the world by our standards: rather like a subway map, it tells you how to get where you're going, and what the stops along the way are, without necessarily relating anything that is on the surface or arranging stops on other lines correctly with respect to the line you are taking

The map is so important, and so famous, that there have been several facsimile editions; for more, wonderful online versions can be consulted, such as https://www.euratlas.net/cartogra/peutinger/.

⁜ NAUTICAL MAPS

Nautical charts in the Middle Ages, as today, were stored rolled up. This is perhaps so that when they are spread out for consultation they do not have creases that would interfere with measurements on the map, or cause confusion with the course lines already marked on the chart.

From the thirteenth century onward, European sailors and geogra-

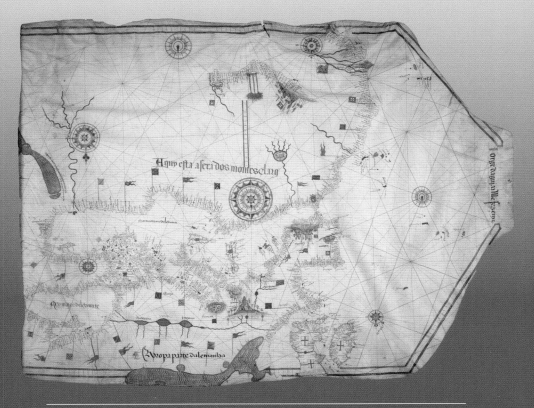

FIG. 3.3

A portolan, or nautical chart, of the Mediterranean area; this is the oldest signed and dated Portuguese chart. An extension to the right bears the name of the maker and the date, "Iorge daguilar Me fezem, lixboano anno domino nostri ihesu Christi 1492." This tab allowed the chart to be rolled on a baton. Measuring about 3 feet by 3 feet 9 inches, the chart, within a red and green border, shows the coastline of the Mediterranean, the Black Sea, and western Africa, alternating place names with black and red ink for legibility. Prominent cities are illustrated and labeled (Lixbona [Lisbon], Gra[na]da, Paris, Genoa, Venexia [Venice]). Flags and coats of arms indicate political affiliations. The African coast, particularly important in this age of exploration, continues, after reaching the bottom of the map, to the right above, apparently in the center of the continent. There are elaborate compass roses, some with the names of the winds; and a series of lines emanating from them in red, and green. There is a certain vagueness around the edges of the map. New Haven, Beinecke Rare Book and Manuscript Library 30cea/1492.

phers produced what are called portolan maps (named for the *portolani*, the pilots who used them), charting nautical seaways for mariners. In the fifteenth and sixteenth centuries, called the Age of Exploration, such charts were considered state secrets by the competing powers of Portugal and Spain.

All portolan charts feature compass roses, oriented to the magnetic north pole and showing the thirty-two headings of the compass. Series of radiating lines indicate lines of bearing.

✤ GUIDES

Pilgrimage, going to a holy place for religious self-improvement, was the motivation for much medieval travel. Sometimes it was a trip to the cathedral to venerate the relics of the local saint; at other times the destination was farther afield. Not everybody could travel to the Holy Land, but there were pilgrimage sites throughout the Christian world. Famous among them were the churches of Rome, the shrine of St. James at Compostela in Spain, and that of Saint Thomas Becket at Canterbury (the destination of the pilgrims in Chaucer's *Canterbury Tales*).

Some pilgrims' guides were presented helpfully and effectively on scrolls. Some were based on a map, but at least one surviving example is essentially a long text with illustrations: it is a pilgrim's roll, dated 1417, which records the pilgrimages of a certain Peter of the Cross (Petrus de Cruce) first in the Holy Land and then, in a separate text, visiting venerable relics in Greece, the Balkans, Italy, and elsewhere. It is not clear why this guide is in roll form, but it might have been for portability, and to open easily to the names of the next places on the traveler's itinerary.

Two illustrations show, first, someone, presumably Peter himself, disembarking, in his Dominican friar's habit, in the Holy Land; in the other, another figure, also thought to be Peter, encounters wolves and snakes with Saint Michael the Archangel protecting him from atop a mountain.

There are many places to visit in the Holy Land, and many good reasons to do so for a Dominican friar. The Dominicans, with their characteristic hooded white tunic worn under a hooded black cape, are also known as the Order of Preachers, and were founded by the Spanish Saint Dominic. The order, officially recognized in 1216, sought to preach to the broad populace. Its rapid spread made it highly influential, along with the Franciscan order, in the religious life of the later Middle Ages.

Peter of the Cross, who commissioned this scroll, was a *conversus*, a layperson who joined the Dominican order. He must have had considerable resources to afford his three voyages to the Holy Land, whose sites are listed in detail on his scroll.

There is something perhaps a little calculating in Peter's recommendations for pilgrimage: those who visited certain holy places received a plenary indulgence (complete remission of sins, with no time in Purgatory). These valuable sites are marked on the scroll with a red cross. Visiting certain other places got the pilgrim seven years and seven times forty days' time off from the pains of Purgatory. Why you would need the latter if you had a plenary indulgence is a calculation that Peter does not explain. Indulgences were used to encourage holy life, of course, and they were useful in encouraging religious behavior such as joining crusades, building and supporting churches, and going on pilgrimage.

It was Constantine's mother Helen who had traveled to the Holy Land in search of the relic of the Cross of Jesus, which she recovered after many trials and brought back to Rome. Helen is thus the model for later pilgrims, who emulate her devotion to the holy places of Christ's life by visiting historical holy sites. Peter of the Cross's pilgrimage is in two parts: first, a detailed list of where to go in the Holy Land and Egypt, with indications of where plenary indulgences are to be obtained. The second text describes holy sites in Europe, but in a more haphazard way. Italy and the eastern Mediterranean seem to have good, perhaps firsthand coverage; the voyage continues through Dalmatia and around Italy, continuing in France, with mentions of Germany, Spain, and Portugal, getting less detailed, and less logical for an itinerary, as Peter's information seems to fade.

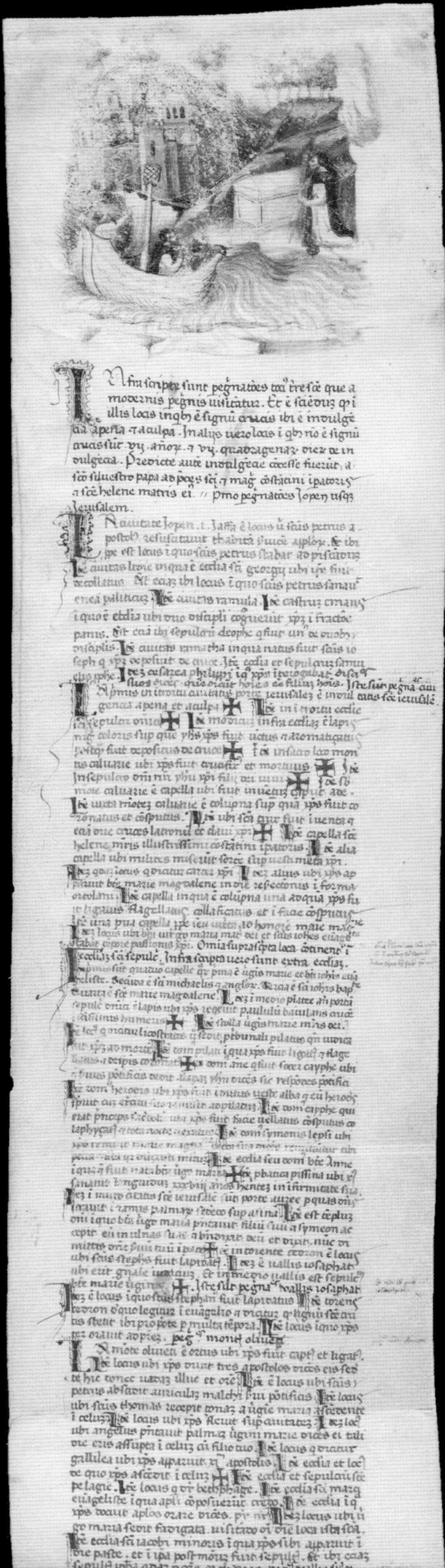

FIG. 3.4A

Detail of a pilgrimage roll, some 5½ feet long and a little over 5 inches wide, showing sites in Egypt and the Holy Land; the text is by the Dominican friar Petrus de Cruce, probably the figure at the top dressed as a pilgrim, who arrives by sea and prays at a shrine.

In red below is an introduction: "Below are written the pilgrimages of the Holy Land which are visited by modern pilgrims. And note that in those places where there is the sign of the cross, there is indulgence from punishment and from sin. But in other places, where there is no sign of the cross, there are seven years and seven times forty days' indulgence. The indulgences mentioned were granted by Pope Saint Sylvester at the request of Emperor Constantine the Great and Saint Helen his mother. The first pilgrimage: from Joppa to Jerusalem."

Then follows a list of places to visit: Jaffa, where Peter raised Tabitha from the dead; Ramula, whose suburb Emmaus was the site of a recognition of the resurrected Jesus; Ramada, where Saint Joseph was born; Cesarea Philippi, etc. The first red cross, accompanied by a rubric in the right margin, notes the pilgrim's entry into Jerusalem. MS Typ 1001 A, Houghton Library, Harvard University.

The illustration contains Latin text at the top:

S l prasenta loca 'q ueneratones scor sunt que ego fra
petrus de cruce conuersus ordis predicator nosemel
s3 bis teriq3 duersis tepor ib3 uidi q pro deuotone mea uisi
taui ut deo placuit omia aute hic hec ordie scribi feci ut
alijs sit quodaz itinerariuz in anno dnice incarnatonis. M°
ccccxvij Indictone. x. die xxvj" mes. Marcij :+

FIG. 3.4B
The second part of the scroll,
originally attached to its end.
Here Peter claims authorship
and authority. The text, in red,
reads: "The abovementioned
places and venerations of the
saints which I, brother Petrus
de Cruce, a lay brother of
the Order of Preachers (the
Dominicans) saw, not twice,
but at three different times, and
visited for the devotion of my
soul that it might be pleasing
to God, I have thus caused all
these things to be written here
in this order, that it might be
an itinerary for others. In the
year of the Lord 1417, the 10th
Indiction, the 26th of March."

The illustration shows two
events described in Peter's
travelogue: his rescue from
poisonous snakes by Saint
Nicholas near Bari (site of
Nicholas's tomb), and from
wolves by Saint Michael the
Archangel at Monte Gargano,
an important Italian pilgrimage
site dedicated to the warrior
Archangel. MS Typ 1001 A,
Houghton Library, Harvard
University.

✥ TIME AS DISTANCE

The examples we've just seen are in scroll form in order to represent distance in a line, as we regularly do in maps. Distance along a line, as used in these maps and guides, can also represent time as we understand from everyday use in familiar kinds of timeline: charts, clock faces, and graphs. Five minutes around a clock is one twelfth of the whole circumference; an inch across the chart or graph represents a year, or a century. Space represents time in written or printed language, and in musical notation, where time unrolls from left to right. The scroll bars at the bottoms of audio and video files tell us how far along we are in time. A timeline, then, can be as long as needed; in a scroll, it can be unbroken. The most frequent uses of this convention in medieval scrolls—using a line to represent time—are in histories and genealogies, where the passage of time is represented by subsequent events or the next generation. In these scrolls, time travels downward, as it were, through the years from some beginning point—Creation, Adam, the first king of England—to the present day.

Peter of Poitiers' Compendium

One of the most frequently copied such histories, or timelines, is Peter of Poitier's *Compendium historiae in genealogia Christi* (Compendium of history in the genealogy of Christ). Although Peter's history is found also in codex form, it often is presented on scrolls like the one shown here, from the first half of the thirteenth century, which allow the genealogical and historical aspects to be physically apparent.

Peter (ca. 1130–1215) was an eminent theologian at the University of Paris and chancellor of the Church of Paris. The education of the clergy was one of the chief purposes of Peter's writings include significant theological commentaries and summaries of his teaching, and he is known to have championed the teaching of poor clerics: the level of literacy among the regular parish clergy may have been fairly low; it was necessary to be able to say the words of the Mass and certain other prayers, but clerical standards were low. The Third Lateran Council (1197), presided over by Pope Alexander III, established several rules to address this: no one could be a parish priest before the age of twenty-five; no one could be ordained priest without some means of support; and every cathedral should appoint a master to teach the clerics and scholars (these cathedral schools were at the origins of later universities). The Fourth Lateran Council (convened in 1215) continued to be concerned with these matters (among others).

It is in this atmosphere that Peter's *Compendium* appeared. As chancellor, Peter headed the schools that were being assembled into the University of Paris. In addition to being a theologian, then, Peter was a leading educator. Not everybody agrees that he was the author of the *Compendium*, though most medieval scribes and readers believed so, and the *Compendium*'s purpose certainly fits with Peter's own concern for the limited education of many of the clergy.

The *Compendium* presents a greatly abbreviated version of biblical history, and includes illustrations and diagrams to facilitate study and memorization. It is intended as a study and teaching aid, a quick guide to the chronology of biblical history, with theological implications explained along the way. The author explains in an introduction that he intends to help students who are prevented from mastering biblical history because of its length, and because they are too poor to own books:

> Considering both the prolixity of history and its difficulty, and the ignorance of students . . . and wanting to provide a little package they could use to retain the narrations of history in memory, I attempted a sequence from the holy Fathers from whom the origins of Christ from the Levites and the royalty of the tribe might be learned, and to reduce their works into a small tract. Because of the sheer quantity of material, and because figures for the eyes are a delight to the soul, it is easy to commit to memory what the eye sees, and convey what is useful to all readers. . . . And so, beginning with Adam, I laid out the order of patriarchs, judges, kings, prophets, and the priests of their times up to Christ and unto our times.

Peter's history begins at Adam and continues to the birth of Christ and the appearance of his twelve apostles. In almost all versions it includes numbers of diagrams, some of them historical and others figurative, which facilitate the use of the scroll as a teaching device and help in memorization. There are also illustrations of persons, like Noah and Alexander the Great, who are not relatives of Christ but figure somehow into the story being told.

The oldest of the surviving scrolls, shown here, actually shows Peter dictating the text to a scribe. His introduction, quoted above in my translation, is written between them; it introduces the summary chronicle that follows, beginning with the creation of the world.

The history is laid out in figures. A genealogical line of descent runs down the center of the document, from Adam and Eve through King David and down to Joseph, husband of Mary. The text is secondary in that it is arranged in whatever space is left free after the fairly complex drawings are executed. In addition to portraits of the major figures of history (with intrusions from nonbiblical history, like Alexander the Great, who appears in his role as the victor over Darius of Persia and conqueror of the great Persian kingdom that figures importantly in biblical history), there are genealogical connections from generation to generation, and many other indications of descent and relationship.

Besides the figures from history, the scroll includes useful diagrams such as the layout of Noah's Ark, the forty-two encampments of the Israelites as they crossed the desert, the arrangement of their tents with the tabernacle at the center, and a circular plan of Jerusalem. The scroll ends with the Twelve Apostles, with the addition of Saint Paul.

The six ages of the world enumerated by Saint Augustine for teaching purposes are diagrammed. The first covers the time between Adam and Noah from the creation to the flood; the remaining ages incude (2) Noah to Abraham; (3) to David; (4) to the Babylonian exile; (5) to the time of Christ; (6) to the early church and Peter's medieval era. These echo the six days of creation.

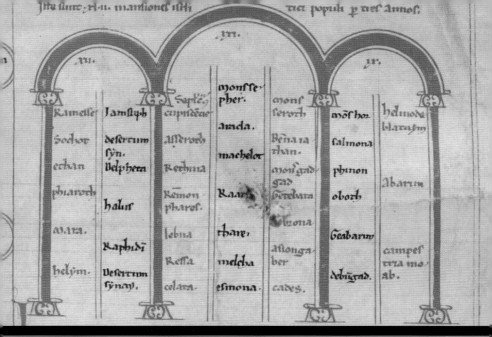

FIG. 3.5A

Two details from Peter of Poitier's *Compendium*, which is arranged as a series of diagrams, with connections or genealogical descent, and with diagrams of events, places, and so on. It is clear from the layout that the drawing comes first, and that the text is fitted in spaces that are available.

A. The forty-two encampments of the Israelites after they left Egypt and traveled in the wilderness; the three arches represent the three years of their journey. The encampments begin at the top of the leftmost, red column, with Rameses and Succoth (Exodus 12:37), and conclude at the lower right with the Plain of Moab (Numbers 22:1).

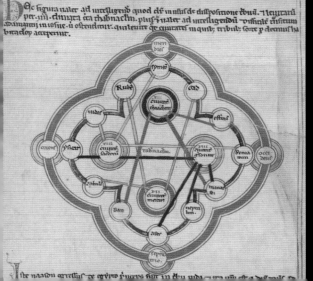

FIG 3.5B The diagram of the position of the Israelites around the central Tabernacle during their journey, as detailed in Numbers 2:4, is in a quatrefoil with circles representing the locations of the twelve tents of the tribes of Israel around the periphery. The roundels are connected with colored lines to show relationships between locations and tribes. The twelve tribes are in circles connected with a blue line. There are four primary circles in the center of the diagram, which represent the four Levitic dynasties (clockwise from top: Kohathites, Gershonites, Merarites, Priests, with Moses and Aaron). The outer red quatrefoil, which holds four gold roundels, is labeled with the four cardinal points. MS Typ 216, Houghton Library, Harvard University

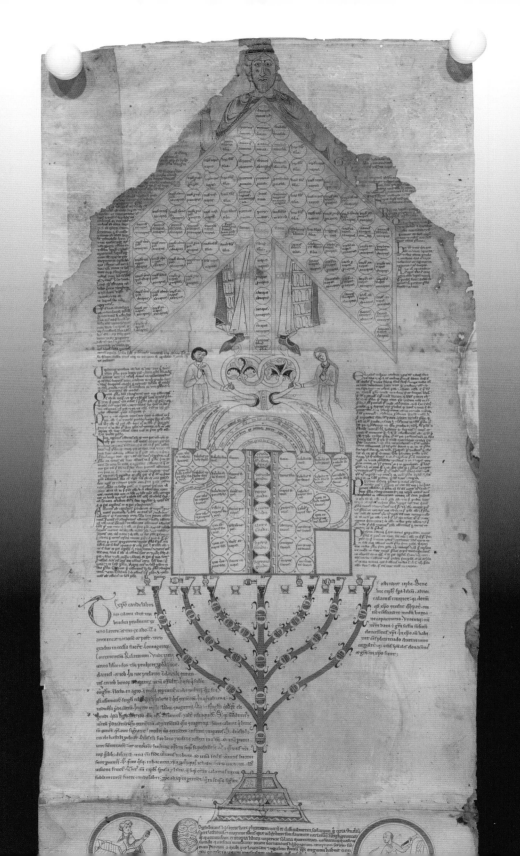

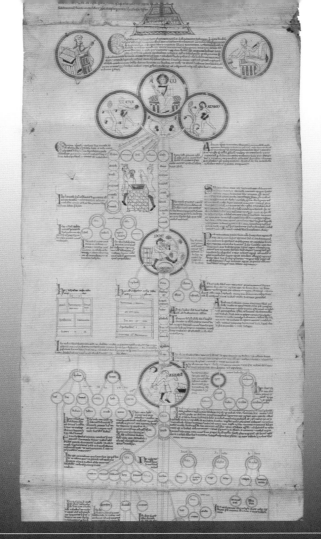

FIG. 3.6

A. *(Opposite)* This version of the *Compendium* begins with pedagogical material not part of Peter's text but useful for the education of clergy. At the top is a table of consanguinity—how closely people are related, and who may not be married to whom. It takes the form of circles arranged in a triangle, with the head, arms, and feet of the figure of Adam—the ancestor of all—as its corners. The person from whom relationships are measured is an unmarked circle in the center.

Adam and Eve appear holding on to the intertwining vines of the kinship chart. Next follows a seven-branched candelabrum, with commentary on either side. The central branch represents Christ incarnate; three branches on either side—before and after the incarnation—represent the three orders of the faithful, arranged in a hierarchy: the clergy, associated with Noah; the continent, with Daniel; and the married, with Job. These orders are not equal, but each derives from the main stem and each shares equally in the light of Christ. Below the candelabrum begins the *Compendium* with the figures of Peter and his scribe. MS Typ 216, Houghton Library, Harvard University.

B. *(Above)* In this second of six membranes, a triple roundel shows God the Father (unusually, his nimbus has a cross) with Adam and Eve; below them on the left are Cain and Abel. Lower are Noah harvesting with his red hat; below him on the left two diagrams of the layout of the Ark (according to Moses and to Josephus); each has compartments for men and birds; tame and wild animals; storerooms, privies, and bilge. Lower still, the angel prevents Abraham from sacrificing his son Isaac. MS Typ 216, Houghton Library, Harvard University.

Histories

✤ CHRONIQUE UNIVERSELLE DU MONDE

Some of the largest medieval scrolls that survive are versions of a fifteenth-century French history of the world created along the lines of Peter's *Compendium*. This history, the *Chronique Universelle du Monde* (Universal chronicle of the world), is written in parallel stories, including history down to the time of the writing of the scrolls. (Twenty-nine of these scrolls survive.) Almost all of them were made in France, although one may be of English origin, and all are illustrated. They combine sacred and secular histories. The Bible, ancient Greek and Roman history, as well as contemporary history (mostly French, with an occasional digression to England) were woven together, sometimes separated into parallel columns, so that history unrolls in a vertical timeline combining text and illustrations.

The Ages of Man, known also from Peter's *Compendium*, are followed by explanations of how the earth was peopled after the Tower of Babel and how the Trojans were descended from Japheth (Noah's third son, from whom in turn descend the kings of France and England); then follow ancient history, popes, emperors, and kings.

The text here begins with the creation, in two columns, then adds to biblical history the stories of ancient Egypt, Greece, and Rome in columns to the right. Eventually, there are four columns: the Bible and the Papacy; the Roman and Holy Roman Empires; France; and England. (England is treated as an aspect of French history, of course—this is a France-oriented text, after all.) Towards the end, the chronicle concentrates almost exclusively on the recent history of France, with clearly French points of view with respect to events like the Hundred Year's War; some scrolls continue as far as the coronation of Louis XI in 1461.

We can only guess the use of such magnificent scrolls. Of course, they are useful for teaching history, as well as for comparing events in different parts of the world. Some of them belonged to noble families, who perhaps were proud of their relationship, or acquaintance, or kin-

FIG. 3.7

A copy of the *Chronique universelle* (Universal chronicle), unrolled during restoration.
MS Typ 41, Houghton Library, Harvard University.

ship, with the royal family, and wanted to be able to point it out. Others are not so magnificent, and may have a more straightforward purpose of record keeping or education. The enormous size and grand illustration of most of them, however, makes their practical employment hard to imagine.

Genealogies

Royal genealogies also survive on scrolls. A few of them are French, but most are English. As noted, the scroll is an ideal format for tracing a direct line of descent—a list of popes, emperors, or one's ancestors. But everyone familiar with genealogy knows that the branching aspect of relationships suggests a figure more like a tree than a line. So most genealogical scrolls are centered on a direct line because their makers are

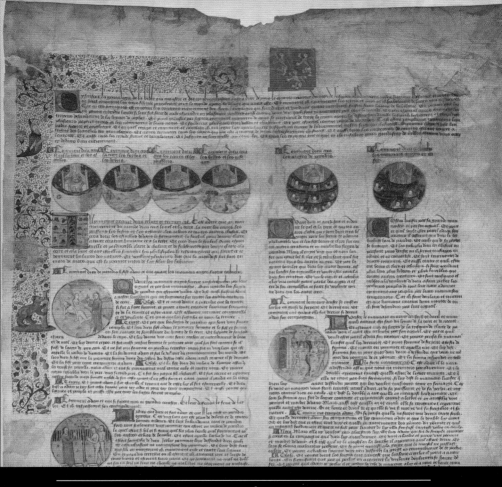

FIG. 3.8A

Chronique anonyme universelle du monde (Anonymous universal world chronicle),
fifteenth century. This is one of twenty-eight versions of this text. The scroll is
decorated at top and left with foliage, animals, and birds, in the manner of a codex.
To the right are the arms of the Flemish Gavre de Liederkerke family, evidence of
its early ownership.

The introduction indicates the vast sweep of the history to follow: biblical
history, ancient history, popes, emperors, and kings of France. The roundels to
the left show the creation: (1) Heaven and Earth, sun and moon; (2) plants and
trees; (3) waters and fishes; (4) animals and birds. On the right are the creation of
the angels and the expulsion of evil angels into hell. The story of Adam and Eve
follows, with six roundels depicting their creation, temptation, and downfall. MS
Typ 41, Houghton Library, Harvard University.

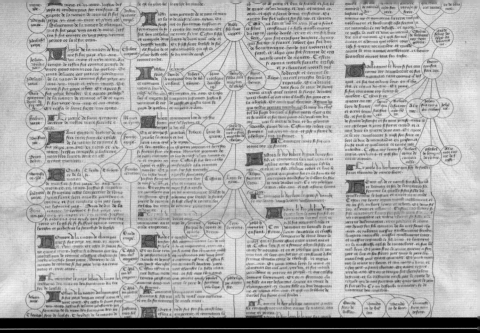

FIG. 3.8B

Another section from the same scroll. Four columns give parallel histories: popes at left, Roman (and Byzantine) emperors, kings of France, and kings of England. On the right a red line connects kings even when they are not related; the last king in this picture is Harold, who "lost all of England and was killed" in 1066). The red line connects him directly with William the Conqueror, to whom he was not related. Reading leftward, Harold is roughly aligned with Louis the Stammerer, king of France (877–879); further left is Jovian, Roman emperor in Constantinople (363–364), and left-most is Pope Sixtus III (432–440). The columns are parallel, but the chronology is not!

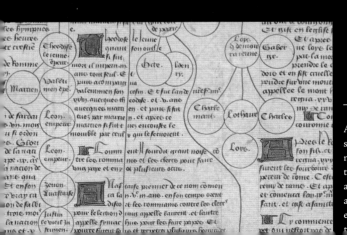

FIG. 3.8C

A detail from the section above, showing how the red circles must have been drawn first, the connection lines second, and then the text, filling in but avoiding the drawing. Note especially how the text dodges the vertical line at left.

interested in a succession of individual figures, rather than all possible linkages.

It's a particularly English tradition to make genealogical scrolls of their kings—perhaps for the same reason that there are so many English heraldic and archival rolls. Whatever the reason is, it's an English characteristic. More than a hundred genealogical scrolls dating from the thirteenth century to the sixteenth century and later survive today.

FIG. 3.9

A portion of this roll shows the last Danish king, Harthacnut, son of Cnut the Great, who conquered England in 1016. Harthacnut was succeeded by Edward the Confessor ("Seint Edward"), whose line of succession from his father, Ethelred the Unready, dodges around the Danish interruption. Edward had no children, and at his death in 1066 he was succeeded by Harold Godwinson; shortly thereafter Harold was defeated at the Battle of Hastings, resulting in the period of Norman rule that began with William the Conqueror. MS Typ 11, Houghton Library, Harvard University.

FIG. 3.10

A roundel showing "William the Bastard," also known as William the Conqueror, who succeeded Edward the Confessor as king after a struggle culminating in the Battle of Hastings in 1066. (William is called "the Bastard" mostly in non-Norman sources, giving a clue as to the origins of this scroll.) He was the son of the unmarried Robert I, Duke of Normandy, and the duke's mistress Herleva. His line of descent from the Norman dukes is above him on the scroll, leading to him by a red line. He is shown holding a sword, and rests his feet on the outline of the red roundel. The commentary to the left identifies him as "William bastard and warrior, conquered the realm of England by battle with Harold. . . ." The texts are in Anglo-Norman, a sort of French used in post-conquest England. MS Typ 11, Houghton Library, Harvard University.

One splendid roll from the thirteenth century shows the genealogy of kings of England from Aethelstan (894–939) to Edward I (1239–1307). It is made of six membranes, thirteen feet long and some ten inches wide. The scroll is essentially organized around the diagram, with commentary written in available spaces. More than a hundred polychrome portraits, in roundels drawn with a compass, are connected with zigzag bands. The largest roundels, placed along a vertical center axis, are imaginary portraits of monarchs: twenty-two kings and three dukes of Normandy. Smaller roundels show relations: children, spouses, and others. Each roundel contains a name, and additional information may

FIG. 3.11 A AND B
Two sections of a thirteenth-
century genealogy of the kings
of England, showing at right
William the Bastard (William the
Conqueror), from a thirteenth-
century genealogy of the kings of
England. Below William are his
nine surviving children: Robert
Curtehose, William, Richard,
Henry, [Matilda his wife, "la
duchesse"?], Cecily, "abbesse" of
the Trinity in Caen, wearing a veil,
Constance "la duchesse" (these
last two have been scraped and
rewritten) and two ("the fourth"
and "the fifth"), who died.

William (Rufus, or the Red) is
picked out of the line of children
by a green line and reappears in a
red roundel as "William le Rous,"
King William, who died in the New
Forest from an arrow shot. He was
succeeded by his brother Henry
(yellow line of descent), usually
called Beauclercq, here "Henri
le clerc"). Henry was married to
Matilda, queen of Scotland (long
green line of descent up the side),
and things get very complicated,
until Stephen (another son of
William the Conqueror—red line)
seizes the throne. No wonder so
many explanations are required in
the margins.

The diagram represents three
kinds of relationship: most frequent
and most important is the parent-
child relationship, but it also
represents marriage (here, that of
Henry I "le clerc" and Queen Matilda
of Scotland); in certain instances
a single person appears more than
once—for example, Henry appears
first as one of William's children,
and again as king (and husband
and father). MS Typ 11 Houghton
Library, Harvard University.

be included outside the circle, like the spousal name of a married woman, or a title, such as "abbess."

This scroll is essentially oriented vertically, with kings aligned one above another at the center. But there are other orientations too. Horizontal lines show approximate contemporaries, like William's children, but in an order that is only partly chronological; first the men, then the women, then those who didn't survive—each group in chronological order. And the commentary diverts the viewer to the side of the scroll to read explanations of historical events such as how this person came to be in this place, and other useful material; taken together it comprises a sort of written history of which the genealogical diagram is the skeleton.

The scrolls in this chapter have in common what Edward Tufte, the Yale expert on data representation, calls the visual display of quantitative information. Their purpose is not really, however, to display specific distances—exactly how far it is to Rome or Jerusalem—or exact amounts of time between Adam amd Moses or between one English king and the next. But they do provide an orientation of direction: traveling along a line represents the passage of distance or of time. We are used to this in many modern forms, and it retains its usefulness.

Many scrolls may have been used in practice as maps that could be unrolled to the section needed at various points of the journey, but these maps, if they existed, have not survived or been rediscovered. This is no surprise, of course, given the wear and tear that they would surely have suffered and the possibility that they might have been discarded when a trip was completed. It is surely no accident that the chronicles, genealogies, and linear maps that survive are beautifully decorated. It's the decoration that got saved, not the practical use of using a scroll to look up an early king of England or a descendant of Noah.

Representing space or time by a line or a physical distance has obvious advantages, and we see them in these scrolls. But like any translation, they are imperfect. You have to do a lot of scrolling; you can't see the whole extent unless you unroll the whole scroll. And it's difficult to get everything right. The genealogical scrolls are fine when son follows father in regular succession, but when invaders, usurpers, or conquerors come into the picture—especially if they are descended from an earlier person on the line—the representation can get difficult. For the histories, it is hard to keep simultaneous events simultaneous. Even though the *Chronique universelle* shows simultaneous histories in parallel columns, the parallel places are seldom simultaneous; it doen't work out that an important event requiring reporting in Rome is accompanied by an equally important event, requiring the same amount of space, in Byzantium. Approximation, at the least, has to be part of this effort. But the scroll format shows us more, and more relationships, with fewer interruptions, than would be possible in the successive pages of a codex.

CHAPTER 4

Performers' Scrolls

f you were a performer, you might well have opted for a scroll in the event that you needed to refer to a poem, a dramatic part, or a musical notation while you performed. A scroll can be small and unobtrusive, it can be unrolled as little or as much as necessary, and it need only have the material a performer needs. Various kinds of scroll for poets, for actors, and for musicians survive from the Middle Ages. Sometimes they are very handsome, as in the case of a few musical scrolls; and sometimes they are very plain, meant to be a temporary expedient until the part or the poem is learned.

Actors' Roles

> *Snug:* Have you the lion part written? Pray you, if it be, give it me, for I am slow of study.
> *Quince:* You may do it ex tempore, for it is nothing but roaring.
> A MIDSUMMER NIGHT'S DREAM, ACT I, SCENE 2

For medieval plays, moralities, mysteries, and farces, it seems to have been common to give each actor his part written out sepa-

FIG. 4.1

(*Opposite*) The figure of Christ enthroned, surrounded by symbols of the four evangelists, from the Stavelot Bible, late eleventh century. London, British Library Additional M 28106-28107. © The British Library Board / The Image Works.

rately, often on a scroll that could be held inconspicuously. In later times, the scroll itself became associated with the part, so that we now refer to parts as actors' roles.

It's no surprise that there are not many surviving examples of actors' scrolls, since presumably once the "role" is learned, the "roll" is discarded. They were not intended as archival or display items: on the contrary, they were to be hidden in the hand. Generally they contained only one role, with cues from the end of another actor's part for each speech.

Sometimes the director's copy, including the various speaking parts but also stage directions, descriptions of sets, and so on, was kept on a scroll. The most famous of these is one dating from about 1350, now in Frankfurt, Germany, containing directions, texts, and music for a two-day-long passion play. It opens a fascinating window onto the workings of a citywide undertaking. Essentially a series of cues and stage directions, the scroll contains the beginning of each speech given, but not the whole thing (presumably, each actor had his own version). The directions are given in red in Latin, but the speeches are mostly in German, except for the places where there is a scriptural quotation or the singing of a chant in Latin. This scroll is a combination of promptbook and stage director's manual. Putting it all together must have been an enormous task, sometimes rather like directing traffic.

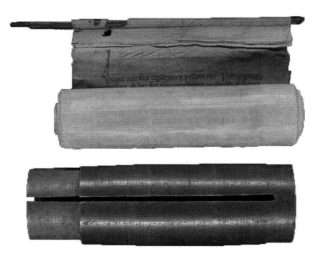

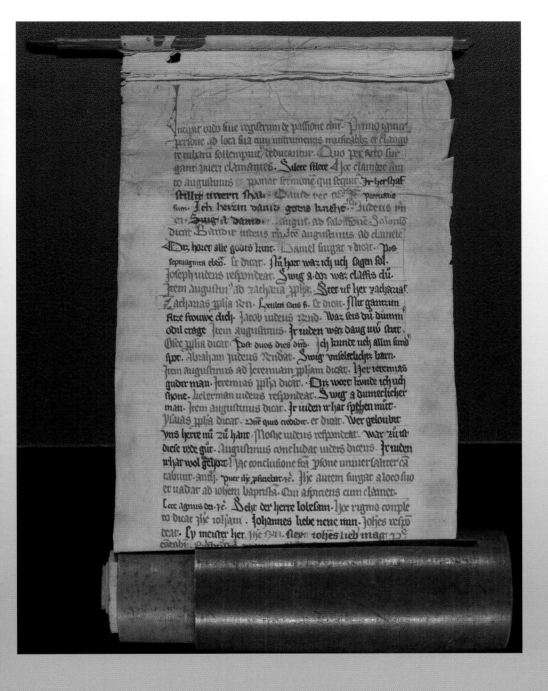

The Frankfurt Director's roll, mid-fourteenth century. The red Latin text gives directions for a long passion play in German; the actors' parts are in black ink. The beginning of the text reads: "Here begins the order or the register of the Passion of the Lord. At first the actors are solemnly led to their places with musical instruments and with the clangor of trumpets. When this is done, some boys arise and shout: 'Be silent! Be silent!'" Frankfurt am Main, Universitätsbibliothek Johann Christian Senckenberg, MS Barth 179.

Making scrolls for the actors in a play must have been a complicated
process when the play was a large one like the Passion play of Frankfurt. We have one instance of trying to keep the play itself secret, as may
indeed have been customary, while preparing the necessary materials
for a city-sponsored mystery play. In 1510, the city fathers of the city of
Valence, in southern France, decreed, in official-sounding Latin,

> . . . that the composition of the scrolls for the 'History of the Three Mar-
> tyrs' should be given to Master Aymarius of Quercus . . . who for an
> agreed price promised on his oath to return and give in the scrolls early
> on the tenth day hence, and to keep secret the original, which is written
> in four quires of paper and contains 102 written folios, and to return it
> with the scrolls on the appointed day.

Another lucky survival is the role of Orlando in Robert Greene's
play "The Historie of Orlando Furioso," published in London in 1594,
and based on Ludovico Ariosto's 1532 Italian romance. *Orlando furioso*
(Mad Orlando, or perhaps Raging Roland) is one of the most significant
works of European literature, influencing not only Greene but writers in
many languages. It is a rollicking tale of Charlemagne's knight Roland
and his adventures in the war between the Christians and the Saracens.
An expansive and discursive poem about love, duty, and chivalry, the
play features sea monsters and flying horses, and ends when Orlando's
lovesick madness is cured by a trip to the moon. Several wonderful and
famous subplots provide material for many adaptations.

Greene sold his play first to the Queen's Players and, while they were
touring the country with it, he sold it again to the Lord Admiral's Men; it
was acted in open-air theaters like Shakespeare's Globe. Edward ("Ned")
Alleyn was the star of the Admiral's Men, famous for his portrayal of
Christopher Marlowe's title characters, including Faustus, Tamburlaine,
and the Jew of Malta. He played the role of Orlando, and his scroll survives (fig. 4.3). It contains only his parts, with cues to let him know when
to begin. This version is somewhat longer than what Greene ultimately
published in 1594, although it is impossible to say whether it was embroi-

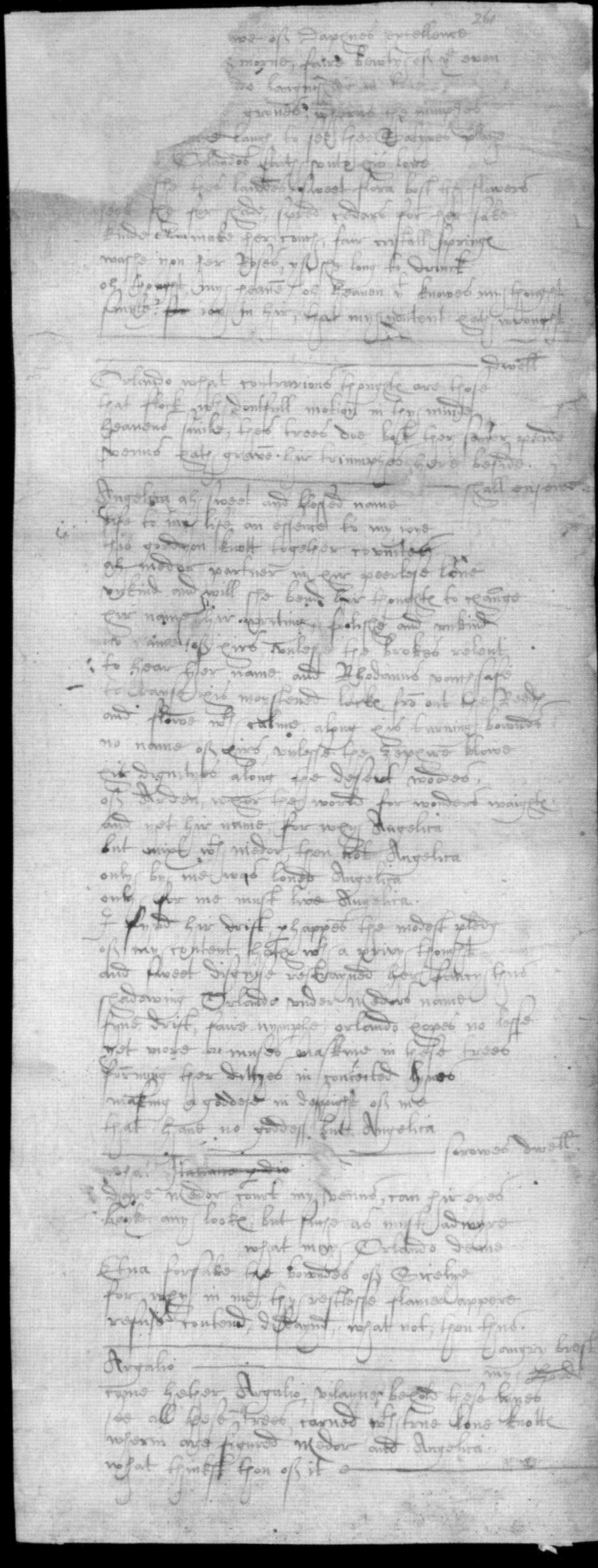

FIG. 4.3

Elizabethan actor Edward
Alleyn's scroll for the part of
Orlando is written on strips of
paper measuring about 16¼ x 6
inches. Horizontal lines separate
the various speeches of Orlando,
with the last few words of the
previous speech serving as cues.
Originally there were probably
fourteen strips pasted together to
form a continuous roll, but they
were separated at some point and
three of them are lost. The person
who wrote out the text had
difficulties transcribing the part:
he got some things wrong and
occasionally left a blank where he
missed something. Alleyn himself
may have supplied words where
necessary. Dulwich College, Ms
1f. 268r detail. ©David Cooper.
With kind permission of the
Governors of Dulwich College.

dered by Alleyn or the published version is a later revision. Alleyn had the part copied, but his scribe couldn't read everything he was copying, and Alleyn added missing words and corrected some errors.

Poetry for Recitation

Medieval poets often used scrolls for recording, and perhaps as aide-mémoires for reciting, their poetry. It is easy to imagine that a poem of moderate length might fit nicely on a single long sheet or strip. Attaching these end to end would result in a roll of several or many poems. Poets in medieval pictures are often shown with scrolls, as though the scroll itself identifies the subject as a poet. For example, the great retrospective manuscripts of poetry, like the famous Manesse manuscript, feature illustrations in which most of the poets are depicted holding scrolls—or at least long strips, but almost never a codex.

✣ NOTKER'S POEMS

From an early medieval poet we have firsthand descriptions of using scrolls in the composition of poetry. Notker the Stammerer, a monk of the monastery of Saint Gall in Switzerland (ca. 840–912), is now known for his *Liber hymnorum* (Book of hymns), a collection of poems designed to be sung. In the preface to it, Notker explains how he came to compose his poems. He had trouble remembering the difficult long melodies he and his fellows were required to sing. But one day, he was given an idea by a Norman monk who was fleeing the Vikings and had arrived at Saint Gall. This monk had a book in which words were set to the notes of the melodies. This gave Notker the idea to compose poetry that would fit the melodies; remembering the poetry would make it easier to remember them.

Notker describes his early efforts as written on pieces of paper or parchment, and subseqently gathered together into scrolls by his master Marcellus:

When I showed these little verses to my teacher Marcellus, he, filled with joy, had them gathered on scrolls [*in rotulas eas congessit*]; and he gave out different pieces to different boys to be sung. And when he told me that I should collect them in a book and offer them as a gift to some eminent person, I shrank back in shame, thinking I would never be able to do that.

FIG. 4.4
An image of Notker Balbulus, the monk of Saint Gall whose *Liber hymnorum* is a treasure house of medieval poetry and music. Here he is depicted with quill and knife, standard equipment for a medieval scribe. Krakow, Biblioteka Jagiellonska MS Theol. Lat. Qu. 11.

FIG. 4.5 A AND B

Two images of poets from the Manesse Codex, named for the fourteenth-century Nuremberg
family who commissioned the book, also known as the Great Heidelberg Song Manuscript. It
a storehouse of Middle High German lyric poetry. Arranged by poet, each section begins with
a portrait of the author whose works follow. On the left, the thirteenth-century Herr Reinmar
von Zweter is depicted in a moment of poetic inspiration, while two assistants write down his

words, one with a stylus on a wax tablet and the other on a scroll. (Some scholars believe that Reinmar was blind, since he is the only poet in the manuscript depicted with closed eyes.) At the right is Walther von der Vogelweide, the most famous of these poets; their virtuosity in song was dramatized in Richard Wagner's opera *Tannhäuser*. Heidelberg, University Library, MS Palatinus Germanicus 848, f. 87-92).

The assembly of the rolls may have been the act of attaching one single-sheet poem to the end of the previous one. If Notker's first versions were written in a single column on one side of a strip of paper or parchment—like those held by other poets in the Manesse Codex—a scroll would result from attaching them end to end. The individual sheets, or versions of them, could be handed out to individuals for performance. Notker's book of poems was adopted by churches throughout the Latin West. It does not survive in scroll form, and probably was not meant to be preserved in that form. But his poems and their music have survived and served as a model for many later medieval poets and composers.

Most of the surviving sources of Notker's book of hymns are in codex form, and they usually contain musical notation as well as text. The notation is usually written above the words, one musical sign per syllable; but sometimes they are written out as a group in the outer margin beside each poetic line. But it seems clear that Notker did not intend musical notation as part of his book. After all, the whole point, as he says, is to remember long melodies. If he had had the use of musical notation for the melodies, he would not have had such trouble remembering them. Most scholars agree that musical notation as we now know it had not been invented, or at least was not known in Notker's monastery. In a sense, Notker's poems are themselves musical notation: they are a means of bringing a melody back into memory and performing it. Presumably, these melodies were sung without words (which is why Notker had such a difficult time with them), and it may be that his original intention, at least in part, was to recall the words silently but sing the melody aloud, using the words only as a memory aid. Notker's poems survive almost always with music, however. And they have been sung—melodies and words—for centuries, and appreciated for their poetic value.

There are not many surviving poetical scrolls. The reason is surely that, like actors' scrolls, they were ephemeral, designed to be inconspicuous. They are also much easier to carry around than a bound book. And when they are no longer needed—when the poet or actor had learned his role—the scroll could be discarded.

❖ HELEN AND GANYMEDE

A dialogue poem called *Altercatio Ganimedis et Helenae* (The debate between Ganymede and Helena) survives on a long strip of parchment from the late twelfth century. At 270 lines long, the poem is a discussion, or debate, between the handsome Ganymede—the most beautiful of mortals—and Helen of Troy about human sexuality—specifically, whether women or men make better sexual partners for men. (It seems nobody was concerned about good sexual partners for women.) The debate takes place before the pagan gods at Olympus, who ultimately make a judgment in favor of Helen. The characters speak alternately, their speeches marked, dramatizing the dispute using this scroll.

In medieval literature love is found mostly in the lyrical poetry and songs written in the vernacular, in Old French, Old Occitan, and other languages. Long texts about theology or about warfare and heroism—that is, about the relationship of man to God, or of man to man, occupied much of human writing. But the personal relationships between men and women are a subject for poetry.

Gay literature was far from unknown in the twelfth century, even though the Church condemned same-sex relationships. But this poem was probably the most widely read text on same-sex love; and it survives in many copies. The nature of the arguments, having to do with God, creation, intelligence, grammar ("a masculine noun and a masculine adjective agree," says Ganymede), and much else, is a sort of scholastic tour de force, like those of many another debate poem. But this one has a lasting effect, and the name "Ganymede" came to be synonymous with the male beloved of another man.

Debate poetry was a staple of the literature of the Middle Ages, and it flourished in the twelfth century. Other examples include debates about the relative virtues of wine and beer, summer and winter, and owls and nightingales.

Musicians' Scrolls

"A lady claims a missal worth twenty shillings, a manual worth 6d. 8d., and *two rolls of songs* worth sixpence and twopence respectively, which were snatched from her on the king's highway between Boughton and her home at Wereham on Easter day 1282."

Musicians, like poets, might have used scrolls when they performed. Indeed, many of the poetic texts of the Middle Ages were meant to be sung, like the hymns of Notker or the poems of the Manesse Codex.

Scrolls of songs were evidently useful to amateurs like the lady of Wereham; and they were used also by performing poets and musicians. Scrolls containing poems that are sung are musical scrolls, whether or not they contain musical notation.

Such an example is a scroll originally from Picardy, with the texts of a number of songs in Old French. It might have been intended for practical use, since it was small enough to hold in the hand. It does

---

FIG. 4.6

(*Opposite*) A Debate About Sex. A poetic scroll containing the dialogue poem *Altercatio Ganimedis et Helenae* ("The debate between Ganymede and Helena"). About 22½ inches long and less than 3 inches wide, it looks as though it might once have been rolled around a small baton. About a quarter of the roll is shown. In the right margin are indications for changes of speaker: Helena and Ganymede. At the top, slits probably show where the scroll was attached to a baton; between the slits are the letters of "Helena." The dialogue here is written in couplets of the kind often used by the student-poets called Goliards. (Poems of that kind are now familiar through Carl Orff's *Carmina Burana*, which sets some such medieval poems to music.) The text, begun on the other side of the roll here continues:

Cum plasmator hominis hominem formaret
Studuit ut feminam viro plus ornaret
Ut ad nexum femine virum invitaret,
Et ne plus quam feminam virum vir amaret.

(When the creator formed man
He took care that the woman should be more comely
That he should be attracted to the ties of woman
And that a man should not love a man more than a woman.)

MS Lat. 198, Houghton Library, Harvard University.

not contain any musical notation, but its poems have musical notation in other sources. It is of course possible to sing a song whose tune one knows without needing musical notation; often the words by themselves are enough.

There are, in fact, very good reasons for *not* including music on a scroll of songs. Musical notation takes up space, for one thing. For each line of text, there is a line of music above it, so that the document takes up twice as much parchment if it contains musical notation. And for the songs in this particular scroll, musical notation would be repetitive, since such songs are written in stanzas, each stanza sung to the same music. Sometimes manuscripts of French songs do contain musical notation,

FIG. 4.7
A picture of three clerics singing from a scroll. In a brilliant 1997 article, the scholar and musician Christopher Page showed that the scroll represents a three-voice polyphonic motet *Zelo tuo langueo/Reor nescia.* From the early-fourteenth-century Howard Psalter, from East Anglia. This is not the only image of such part-singing; there are others, mostly associated with this text, the beginning of Psalm 97 (Cantate Domino canticum novum [O sing unto the Lord a new song]). Perhaps the inclusion of up-to-date polyphonic music is a representation of a new song. London, British Library MS Arundel 83, f. 63v. © The British Library Board / The Image Works.

but even then the notation is normally given only for the first stanza; the singer is expected to adjust the music to all the following stanzas.

There were probably many more musical scrolls than those that survive. Some are known to us from their descriptions in inventories. The parish church in Branscomb, England, lists among its possessions in 1307 "Unus rotulus de cantu organico magnus et longus" [A large and long scroll of instrumental music—or perhaps organ music? Or the type of vocal music known as *organum?*]. It's hard to imagine music for instruments—or music for organ—being played from a scroll, even if the instrument can be played with one hand. The scroll must be a sort of record, for consultation but perhaps not performance. The Benedictine priory of Saint Peter in Leominster, England, had two scrolls in the late fourteenth century: one with music for three voices (*triplices cantus*) and one with music for two voices (*duplices cantus*). Those rolls might have been intended for singers to use in performance—like the singers in fig. 4.7—and could be a reason for separating the two types of music according to how many singers are needed.

✥ SCROLLS OF MUSIC IN PARTS

Music for more than one singer—that is, music in parts—adds a lot of complexity to musical notation and to musical layout. Many singers may use one scroll, of course, if they can all see it and if they are all singing the same song—singing as a choir in unison. But medieval music is sometimes polyphonic, designed for several different parts to be sung at the same time. This is one of the glorious aspects of Western music, and we have the Middle Ages to thank for its development. But writing it down is complicated, for even if all the singers are singing the same words, they are singing different musical parts; each of the parts must be written out separately. And there is the matter of timing. A choir singing a chant can perhaps figure out by eye contact when to change notes, and keep together without too much difficulty. But several different parts create coordination problems. They *were* solved, in the Middle Ages, by the development of a musical notation that gives not only the notes to be sung, but also the durations of those notes—that is, not only pitch, but also rhythm. Various different techniques were tried, but ultimately it was agreed to give each duration a separate shape, and that is still the method we use today: we know how long a note lasts by what it looks like (a half note, a quarter note, etc.).

A few medieval scrolls survive that preserve some of this highly specialized music, and they are really superb accomplishments, on the cutting edge of the technology of the time. Surely the most elaborate and highly decorated music scroll is one made in 1335, following the installation of the new abbot of the princely and imperial abbey of Stavelot, in modern Belgium. It contains music in three parts for three singers. In the first piece, where the parts all have the same words and similar rhythms, the three parts are written on parallel lines, one above another (in score, as musicians say). In the other pieces, the parts are written separately, using two columns, since each part has separate text and music. For these, two of the parts start in two columns. The right-hand column contains the part called the *duplum* voice, which has fewer words that the *triplum* voice on the left. After the end of the duplum, the tenor (which often has only a few syllables) is written next. It is written below the duplum, but is meant to be sung at the same time: the voices are simultaneous, even though someone used to reading text might assume that they are successive. The triplum starts in the left column and continues until the right column has finished with both voices, after which then the triplum spreads to cover lines that go across the whole parchment, like this:

Triplum . . . .   Duplum . . . .

. . . .

. . . .

. . . .   Tenor . . . .

Triplum continues . . . .

. . . .

. . . .

. . . .

The manuscript begins with *Deus in adiutorium*, the opening text sung every day in church at the office hours. This particular three-voice version is known from a number of other musical manuscripts, all of which continue with pieces called motets—just as this scroll does. Here there are eight motets, four on the front and four on the back. Each side begins at the top, so it is not a question of flipping the scroll over and starting from the other end of the back when the scribe came to the end of the front. Decorated initials embellish the manuscript, starting with a particularly handsome initial D with gold leaf for the beginning.

The front has two motets, in Latin, after the opening piece, which warn of the abuse of clerical and secular power, and two more in praise of the Trinity and the Blessed Virgin. The four motets on the other side are arranged in a similar pattern, even though two of them have texts in French. The roll looks to be a sort of greeting and a warning, a ceremonial presentation object along the lines of those books of advice for new kings and princes, of which there were many in the Middle Ages and Renaissance. Such a book is often called a Mirror of Princes. The most famous of them is Machiavelli's *The Prince*, but it is itself far from typical, since it advises the prince in the context of ruling a state. More typical, perhaps, is Baldassare Castiglione's *The Book of the Courtier*, explaining proper behavior at a princely Renaissance court. Such books have a long tradition going back to classical Greece.

This musical scroll may similarly have been intended for encouragement and advice. But for whom? The scholar Karl Kügle has made an impressive case that this splendid roll, assembled from existing musical pieces yet arranged to carry a larger message, was a present, as well as a sort of warning, to the new abbot of an important monastery. (Four of the motets denounce bad management; four others are religious and optimistic). The new abbot was Winricus de Pomerio. Like his predecessors, he ruled the two magnificent monasteries of Stavelot and Malmédy, and was the prince of the region. Unfortunately, almost nothing survives of either monastery, except for this scroll, a couple of chant books, and one of the most beautiful illuminated bibles of the Middle Ages (see fig. 4.1).

A fragment of what may have been a similar scroll survives in Paris. It is only a fragment, but it's apparent that it is from a scroll. It's difficult to say how long it was, because it is incomplete at both top and bottom, having been used as binding material to protect a set of letters and other much later materials. The scroll contains parts of two motets of the same kind as those on the Stavelot scroll and later (mid-fourteenth-century) music, including further motets and two *chaces* (*chaces* are usually in French and on the subject of hunting, in which one voice imitates another as if chasing it). It is hard to judge much from a fragment, but this scroll, not at all elegantly decorated, seems really to be a musician's object.

Another collection of fourteenth-century motets and other music is written on a scroll because the scroll was close at hand and blank on the back. The front of the document is a record of weekly house repairs and improvements at Bretby Manor, a grand property of John, 2nd Baron Segrave (1256–1325). Segrave was a decorated English war hero who was being rewarded for his efforts on behalf of the king. He was a commander in the first war of Scottish independence, serving under kings Edward I and Edward II and scoring notable victories. (Segrave was also involved in the execution of the Scottish hero Sir William Wallace, and had the unpleasant duty of distributing the severed parts of Wallace's body to various places in Scotland.)

For his services, Segrave was richly rewarded by the English sovereigns. In 1301 Segrave received permission to add crenellations to his house at Bretby, and the record of the work week by week over the course of a little less than a year (1302/3) occupies the front of a scroll that is now fourteen feet long and about eight and a half inches wide; it evidently grew in length over the course of the work.

On the back of the scroll, later musicians wrote a series of Latin motets. It is difficult to know when and where these additions were made, but it must have been in a place where expert musicians were present, not especially likely at Bretby. Some scholars think that the music was added between 1327 and 1337, when the son of John Segrave was a ward of Thomas of Brotherton, Earl of Norfolk and youngest son of King

FIG. 4.8
The beginning of the
beautiful Brussels musical
scroll, made in the early
fourteenth century for the
Abbey of Stavelot. The first
piece in the scroll begins
with a large initial "D,"
beginning the text that three
voices sing together: *Deus in
adiutorium* (O Lord, make
haste to help me). The three
musical lines end together
under the big opening letter.
Then begins a three-voice
piece with different texts
in each voice, so the voices
are written out separately:
Super cathedram Moysi (On
Moses's seat) begins in the
left column. Another voice,
Presidentes in thronis seculi
(Presiding on the thrones of
the ages), begins in the right
column, higher up because
the three parallel voice of
the first piece only continued
halfway across the scroll.
A third voice, the tenor,
begins lower down. Brussels,
Bibliothèque royale, MS
19606.

Edward II; perhaps at Brotherton's estate at Framlingham his musicians added the music on the back of the roll, as part of the education of the young John Segrave, but it is really music for expert performances of multivoice music.

⁜ A SCROLL OF CAROLS

Another treasure for English-speaking musicians is a scroll now at Trinity College, Cambridge. On the front is series of carols for two, three, and four voices, with musical notations. Among the famous pieces here is the so-called Agincourt Hymn, celebrating the victory of the English forces of Henry V over those of France at Agincourt in 1415. (The carol, arranged by William Walton, was part of the sound-track of Laurence Olivier's 1944 film *Henry V.*)

> Deo gratias Anglia redde pro victoria!
> (Thanks be to God! England, give thanks to God
>   for victory.)

> *Owre Kynge went forth to Normandy*
> *With grace and myght of chyvalry*
> *Ther God for hym wrought mervelusly;*
> *Wherefore Englonde may call and cry*
> Deo gratias!

Further stanzas are followed by the refrain *Deo gratias . . .* This form, stanzas with refrain, is standard for the carol, but most of the other carols in the scroll are religious. Many of them make use, sometimes wittily, of a mixture of English and Latin.

Some of these charming carols have taken an important place in celebrations of the Christmas season. They are written for three voices, and in the original versions or later arrangements they are frequently sung by choirs. One of them was revisited in modern form by Benja-

FIG. 4.9

The Agincourt Carol, from the scroll at Trinity College, Cambridge. About 6½ feet long and 6½ inches wide. Written in two parallel lines of music, the words are written below the first and second pairs of lines, after which comes a refrain for three parts (*Deo gratias Anglia, redde pro victoria*). Additional stanzas are written below and to the right. Trinity College, Cambridge MS O.3.58. By kind permission of the Master and Fellows of Trinity College Cambridge.

min Britten in one movement of his *A Ceremony of Carols* for treble voices and harp:

> *Ther is no rose of swych virtu*
> *As is the rose that bar Jhesu.*
> Alleluia.
>
> *For in this rose conteyned was*
> *Heven and erthe in lytle space.*
> Res miranda.
>
> *Be that rose we may weel see*
> *That he is God in personys thre.*
> Pari forma.
>
> *Leave we all this worldly mirth,*
> *And follow we this joyful birth.*
> Transeamus.
>
> *The aungelys sungyn the sheperdes to:*
> *"Gloria in excelsis Deo."*
> Gaudeamus.
>
> [Refrain:]
> *Lullay, lullay, lay, lay, lullay*
> *Mi dere moder, sing lullay.*

On the back of the scroll is a series of prayers for private devotion. These are a later addition to the scroll; it was not the first time that it occurred to someone to put to good use the blank space afforded by the back of a scroll.

Most performers operate without the use of written materials. Acting, singing, reciting—we prefer to have no barrier between the performer and the receiver. Yet sometimes performers, today as in the Middle Ages, want or need a reminder of when the next entrance comes, what the next line of the poem is, or how the song goes. What they used were mostly working scrolls, not precious objects designed to preserve texts for posterity; they are words for occasions of performance. We are lucky that a few of these ephemeral objects have survived, because they provide a window onto the landscape of sound of the Middle Ages.

pres la sainte passion
puis la resurrection
De nře šř iħu crist
et co lescripture no dist

Ceulr qui furent es cielr montes
furent aucuns de plus bontes
Et de maintes religions
Apres les predications
Des apostres et des martirs
En avant lesaint esperis

CHAPTER 5

Private Scrolls: Amulets, Charms, and Prayers

As we have noted, compared to a scroll, a codex is the ultimate compact vehicle for writing. It can be written on both sides of the parchment and it provides instant access to any place in the text. We all use codices every day. Yet in the Middle Ages many scrolls—rather than codices—were made to be portable. Some of them were extracts of longer books that would be awkward to lug around. Others were very private objects, meant to be worn on the body. These were very small, to be held, or even concealed, in the hand while reciting or acting or singing, while some were designed for display on a wall, but movable from place to place. For these purposes, a scroll is actually a practical solution.

Amulets and Charms

An amulet is an object, often worn on the body, that protects its user from some harm or danger. It is, of course, not necessarily a scroll; it might be a medal, a symbol, a figure. Medieval amu-

---

FIG. 5.1A

(Opposite) The beginning of a scroll of the life of Saint Margaret. Here the saint emerges from the belly of the dragon. The scroll, in rhymed French, is followed by a series of prayers. The Morgan Library & Museum, MS M.779.

lets usually consist of a small piece of parchment with writing on one side. Folded or rolled to make them as small as possible, they are often enclosed in some sort of covering and kept close, sometimes to conceal them from authorities (magic and appeals to demons or other deities have always been censured by the church). We are concerned here with rolled scrolls (although the same amulet might be stored in either format).

Amulets seem to have been favored by women in medieval France, England, and the Low Countries in particular. Because they deal with private or secret matters, very few such scrolls survive.

Amulets may take the form of a brief, perhaps magical, apotropaic text. Inscribed with Torah verses, the phylacteries worn by Jews are a sort of amulet; they the mark the wearer as observant. Scrolls as amulets need not be worn on the body, of course. The mezuzah affixed to the doorposts of observant Jewish homes is, in its way, a sort of amulet.

Amulet scrolls to be worn—apart from the Jewish examples just mentioned—generally contain Latin or vernacular texts that usually consist of scriptural citations, prayers, litanies, or instructions for devotions to be performed; sometimes they bear devotional images or names of exotic deities or demons, magic spells, symbols, cryptic vowel series (popular in Hebrew charms), magic squares, acrostics, and palindromes like this:

$$
\begin{array}{ccccc}
S & A & T & O & R \\
A & R & E & P & O \\
T & E & N & E & T \\
O & P & E & R & A \\
R & O & T & A & S
\end{array}
$$

This reads the same forwards and backwards, top to bottom, and is found in inscriptions from ancient times through the Middle Ages. Other amulets bear magical words of Near Eastern origin like ABRAXAS and ABRACADABRA; pentagrams, talismanic seals, and manifestations of Solomonic magic and practical Cabala; or a plethora of rhymes, nonsense words, and spells.

Most of the surviving medieval amulet scrolls have a combination of devotional and amuletic functions—for example, prayers that, if recited, have a certain effect, and religious texts that provide some sort of protection or blessing. Especially in need of protection were those pregnant or in childbirth.

One amulet scroll of the fourteenth or early fifteenth century tried to cover a wide range of dangers, a sort of medieval umbrella policy. Unlike most amulets, it was written by professional scribes on eighty-seven lines and stored tightly rolled, probably in some sort of cloth or leather case. Beginning with a list of the names of God, it continues with extracts from the Bible and elsewhere about being safe from demons and dangers, such as "And you shall cast out demons in my name." It includes a charm based on the so-called Divine Letter (extracted from an apocryphal letter of Jesus), long considered a powerful charm, some strongly worded prayers, excerpts from the Gospels relating to childbirth, "Prayers of St. Sigismund king and martyr against fevers," and finally the opening words of Saint John's Gospel ("In the beginning was the Word . . ."), a text widely believed to have special apotropaic powers. Just before the Gospel selections is the instruction, "If a woman is laboring in childbirth let her place this *breve* under her right breast, and then with God's help and in her faith she will be delivered by "tetragramatio + messias + sother [savior] + emanuel + . . ." [a list of names of God, separated by crosses]. Such a scroll apparently protected the user from almost any eventuality.

The lives of saints were a powerful force in medieval religion as examples of holy living. Saints offered a way to God. You might pray to a saint—the saint for whom you were named, your patron saint, or the saint especially known for being effective in particular circumstances—to intercede with the Virgin Mary or directly with God for the accomplishment of your goal. The lives of saints were read in the liturgy on their feast days.

Many surviving amuletic rolls feature the life of Saint Margaret of Antioch, the patron of women in childbirth, so naturally she was the object of special devotion among women. Margaret was swallowed by the devil in the form of a dragon and cut her way out with her crucifix. She is thus often depicted with a dragon as her attribute (which sometimes causes her to be mistaken for Saint George). Her story, one of resurrection through faith, is easy to see as a figuration of childbirth, and the act of reading her life was thought to be a means of protection and safe delivery for medieval women. Many scrolls featuring the life of Saint Margaret survive, and they often include prayers thought to ensure safety. Although these texts and prayers can presumably be as effective in book form as on a scroll, the physical scroll could be stretched on the woman's body to provide a safe outcome for childbirth. Thus, the object and the words it contained both had prophylactic and apotropaic powers.

Very few of the carrying cases for scroll amulets survive. Most of

FIG. 5.1B
The *capsa*, or box, containing a scroll of the life of Saint Margaret, worn as an amulet around the neck. The scroll within is less than 4 inches wide; its six membranes measure 13 feet long. The figure on the front is Saint Margaret; other figures on the box are Saint Peter and John the Baptist. The Morgan Library & Museum, MS M.1092. Gift of an anonoymous benefactor, 1995.

them were likely cloth or leather bags, so they might not be easily recognized. A life of Saint Margaret in its original ciselé leather box, painted and gilded, with images of saints, is in the collection of The Pierpont Morgan Library in New York.

The roll contained in this box is rather worn, but the library has another Saint Margaret scroll (in a later container) that was made in the fifteenth century and is in very good condition (though worn at the top as almost all scrolls are). At the beginning is an illustration of the saint and the dragon, followed by text in rhymed French verse that ends:

> O prion tous a la pucelle
> Marguerite la demoiselle
> Que pour nous prie son creator
> Quen cest secle nous dont honour
> Et bonnes cuures maintenir
> Affin que puissons parvenir
> Lassus en paradis tout droit
> Dictes amen que ainsi loctroit.
>   Amen

> (Now let us all pray to the young girl,
> Margaret the maiden,
> That she pray for us to her creator
> Who praise her in this world
> And maintain good hearts,
> That we may come straight
> There above in Paradise:
> Say "Amen," that so it may be.
>   Amen)

Then comes a series of prayers in Latin, designed, probably, for the user to pray after reading the French text. After all, the life of Saint Margaret ends with an injunction to prayer.

A Life in Pictures: The Guthlac Scroll

Some scrolls consist only of pictures, such as the remarkable and beautiful object known as the Guthlac scroll. Dating from around 1200, it is a horizontal scroll made up entirely of eighteen adjacent roundels depicting scenes from the life of Saint Guthlac. While it is not an amulet, it is included here because it, too, tells the life of a saint.

Guthlac, who lived around 700, was a soldier who later joined the monastery of Repton, a double monastery of men and women ruled by its abbess. Later he became a hermit, retiring to Crowland, an island in the fens, where he learned to understand the strange speech of its British-speaking demons. He built a simple chapel and cells for his followers, and died there in 714. Aethelbald, king of Mercia, built an abbey on the spot, fulfilling the vow he had made when a vision of Guthlac predicted that he would become king. Crowland Abbey grew to be grand, and Guthlac's shrine attracted many pilgrims.

Commissioned by the abbey, the Guthlac Roll was designed to strengthen Crowland as a place of pilgrimage. The last roundel shows a group of pilgrims crowding to offer gifts at Guthlac's shrine. They are actually major benefactors of the abbey, each bearing a scroll that identifies himself and his gift.

While this scroll has been thought to be a pattern book for stained glass or for sculpture, the round form of the images seems more likely to represent a kind of advertisement for pilgrimage to Crowland Abbey as well as a demonstration of the power of the intercession by its founding miracle-working saint.

✤ PRIVATE PRAYERS

Some prayer scrolls were intended for private devotion as property of an individual (we'll look at scrolls used in official liturgy later). You might carry your prayers with you on a scroll to hold in your hand as you say your prayers, or hang the scroll on a wall or above your prayer

FIG. 5.3

The Guthlac Roll, drawn in ink and tinted with a wash that is mostly green and sometimes yellow, is made of five (probably really four and a half) parchment pieces. This detail, the last of eighteen roundels, is a picture full of scrolls. Benefactors approach the shrine of Saint Guthlac, founder of Crowland Abbey. They are led by King Ethelbald, whose scroll says (in Latin) "I, King Ethelbald, give you the seat of the Abbey with its

appurtenances unburdened and free from any secular exaction." He is followed by Abbot Thurketel and others. Behind the shrine an epileptic is cured during a violent seizure, by ejecting a demon from his mouth. The picture to the left showed Guthlac appearing in a vision to King Ethelbald. British Library, Harley Rolls Y6, f. 18r, ©The British Library Board/The Image Works.

desk to provide material for a concentrated moment of communication with the divine. There are wonderful surviving examples of such scrolls, ranging from elaborate documents for kings to simple texts for ordinary people.

✣ ARMA CHRISTI

A number of late medieval scrolls are devoted to meditation on the instruments of Christ's passion, the objects involved in his torture, crucifixion, and death. The *Arma Christi*, the Arms of Christ, rather like the coat of arms of a nobleman, are symbols of his character. A face of Christ surrounded by instruments (nails, crown of thorns, spear, ladder, etc.) is a common image, which may arise from the legend of the Mass of Saint Gregory, in which the saint prayed for a sign to silence a woman who laughed at mass. In high medieval representations, the sign Gregory was granted was the *Arma Christi*.

A fifteenth-century prayer roll in Latin and English contains a variety of prayers to the *Arma Christi*, several saints, and a cross that is said to be one-fifteenth the length of Christ's body; when worn on the body, the scroll would protect it from evil spirits.

These scrolls often have English verses of devotion to the "Vernicle" (from Veronica, *vera icona*, the Greek words for "true image"). The Veronica soon became the Saint Veronica who wiped Christ's brow with a handkerchief that retained the image of his face.

The poem begins:

> *O vernicle, I honour hym and Þe*
> *Þat Þe made throwo his pruete,*
> *Þe cloth he sete to his face,*
> *Þe prent last per thorow his grace,*
> *His mouth, his nose, his egyen two,*
> *His berde, his here dede al so,*
> *Schilde me fro all Þat in my life*
> *I haf synned with wittes fyfe . . .*

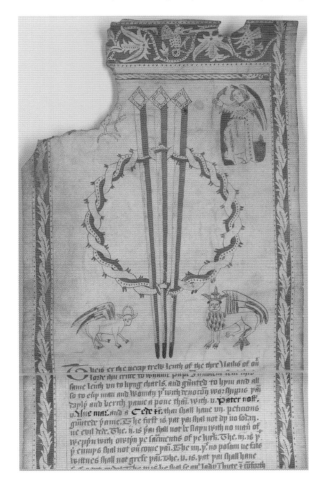

FIG. 5.4
The opening section of a late fifteenth-century prayer scroll. Three nails are flanked by symbols of the four evangelists. The opening text explains that these are the very length of the nails used on the cross of Jesus, and that saying the requisite prayers will protect the user from harm. The roll continues with prayers to a series of saints. New York, The Morgan Library and Museum MS G 39. Gift of the Trustees of the William S. Glazier Collection, 1984.

The verse continues with meditations on the various instruments. Holding the scroll and reading or saying the meditation must have involved physical as well as mental activity.

With regard to physical activity, a scholar has commented about a similar scroll, "The daily handling of this roll, which measures approximately thirty feet in length, must have added greatly to the discipline of private devotion. It is hardly surprising, therefore, that both the handwriting and the decoration indicate by their freshness that the roll has seen little service since its execution in the fourteenth century."

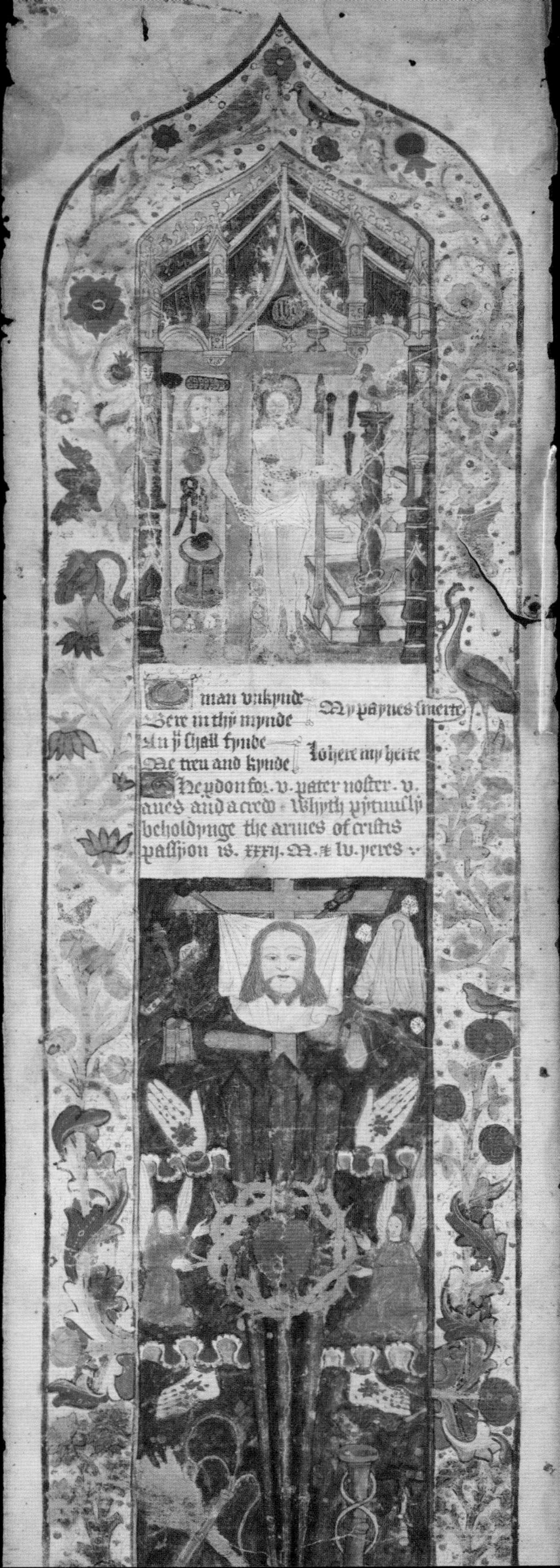

FIG. 5.5
A fifteenth-century English prayer scroll and amulet. The scroll is 5 feet long and 6½ inches wide. The scroll, in addition to serving for devotions, also works as an amulet; if properly used, the opening text explains, the user "shall dye none evyll dethe . . . he shall not be slane with no waking. . . ." At the foot of the veronica with the instruments of the passion is a Dominican friar (?), the user of the scroll, holding in his hand a representation of this very scroll. New Haven, Beinecke Rare Book and Manuscript Library, MS 410.

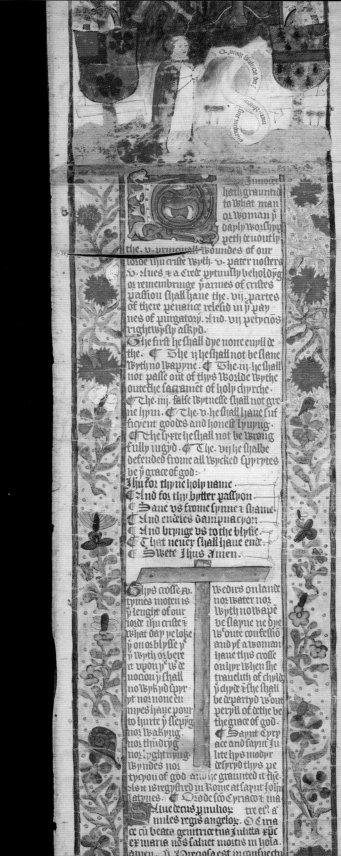

Innocent
hath grauntid
to what man
or woman þ
dayly worlshy
peth dewoutly
the .v. pryncypall woundes of our
lorde ihu criste wyth .v. pater nostere
.v. aues & a crede þytmally beholdyng
or remembrynge þarnes of cristes
passion shall haue the .vij. partes
of there penaunce relesid in þ pay
nes of purgatory. And .vij. petycyos
rightwysly askyd.

The furst he shall dye none euyll de
the. ¶ The ij he shall not be slane
wyth no wapyne. ¶ The iij he shall
not passe out of thys worlde wythe
oute the sacramet of holy chyrche ·
¶ The iiij false wytnesse shall not gre
ne hym. ¶ The .v. he shall haue suf
ficyent goodes and honest lyuyng·
¶ The syxte he shall not be wrong
fully iugyd · ¶ The .vij he shalbe
defended frome all wycked spyrytes
be þ grace of god:·

Ihu for thyne holy name ·
¶ And for thy bytter passyon ·
¶ Saue vs frome synne & shame ·
¶ And endeles dampnacyon ·
¶ And brynge vs to the blysse ·
¶ That neuer shall haue ende ·
¶ Swete Ihus Amen ·

Thys crosse xv
tymes moten is
þ lengyth of our
lorde ihu criste &
what day þe loke
þ on or blysse þ
þ wyth or bere
it vpon yt w de
nocion þ shall
no wykyd spyr
yt nor none en
myes haue pour
to hurte þ slepyg
nor wakyng
nor thudryg
nor lyghtnyng
wyndes nor
tyeyou of god

wedirs on lande
nor water nor
wyth no wape
ve slayne ne dye
ls oute confessio
and yf a woman
haue thys crosse
only þr when she
traueluth of chyld
þ chylde & the shall
be departyd wout
peryll of dethe be
the grace of god ·
¶ Saynt Cypr
ace and saynt Iu
lite hys modyr
desyryd thys pe
and he graunted it the
els is regystred in Rome at saynt Iohn
latynes. ¶ Orode sēē pyracōt ma
Aue decus þ milor te es a
miles regis angelor. O ema
ce cū beata genitrice tua Iulitta ryē
ex maria nos saluet mōtis in hoia
amen · þ Preciosa est in cōspectu

❖ INDULGENCE SCROLLS

A life of penitence and prayer can lead to a swift reunion with God in heaven. So medieval Christians believed, and thus they sought to remove the guilt of their inevitable sin by confession, penitence, and good works. Performing all these tasks was thought to shorten the time that the soul undergoes purification in purgatory, and so it was desirable to obtain indulgences, as they were called, for the good of one's soul. (Recall that in Peter of the Cross's tour of the Holy Land, visits to certain sites gained the pilgrim a certain number of days' indulgence.) Systematized by the Church, the system of indulgences was a way to encourage piety and good works—including contributions to the church—but it could also be abused, as Martin Luther pointed out. Nevertheless, many Christians were very serious about accumulating indulgences for themselves and on behalf of others.

One handsomely decorated indulgence scroll contains prayers to be said by an individual in order to reduce time in purgatory. Written in Latin, perhaps in Germany in the early fifteenth century, it is decorated with flowers, foliage, and animals. It also provides instructions for use: saying the first seven prayers, with Hail Marys and Our Fathers, gets the user 48,040 years and forty-eight days of indulgence, that is, time off from purgatory—provided that they be said with a penitent heart. The same series of prayers, but in Dutch, is found on another *Arma Christi* roll, where the user gains 40,040 and seventy-two days. The Dutch scroll specifies that the user is to meditate on the *Arma Christi*, while the scroll in Latin requires only devout recitation of the prayers.

The prayers themselves are penitential in nature, addressed to Christ as he is hanging on the cross, with crown of thorns and wounds, in the sepulcher, descending to Hell, rising and ascending, as a good shepherd, and at the moment of the separation of his soul from his body. The scroll contains additional prayers on the subject of penitence addressed to Saint Gregory the Great, Saint Mary, a guardian angel, Saint Anne, and Saint Mary Magdalene, which is why Mary Magdalene, a notable penitent, features prominently.

FIG. 5.6
A scroll of prayers in Dutch, for use in meditating on the *Arma Christi*, the instruments of Christ's passion, 7½ inches wide and not quite a yard long. The same prayers, in Latin, are found on a prayer scroll at Harvard (see fig. 5.7). New Haven, Beinecke Rare Book and Manuscript Library, Beinecke MS 1187.

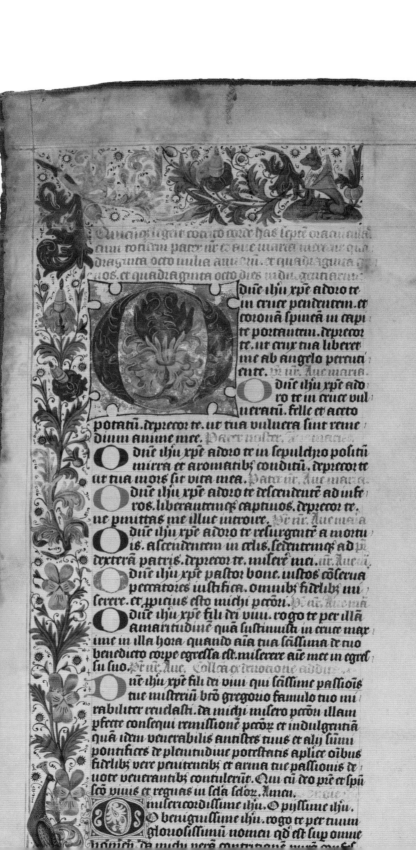

Quicūqꝫ legit coram Arma xpri has septē oraciones
cūm totidē pater nr̄ et Aue maria indebit quadragĩta octo milia annorū. et quadragĩta qn-
nos. et quadragĩta octo dies induł giaꝫ etꝯ

Dn̄e ihū xp̄e Adoro te
in cruce pendentem. et
coronā spineā in capi-
te portantem. depꝛecoꝛ
te. ut crux tua liberet
me ab angelo percuti-
ente. Pꝛ nꝛ. Aue maria.

Dn̄e ihū xp̄e ado-
ro te in cruce vul-
neratū. felle et aceto
potatū. depꝛecoꝛ te. ut tua vulnera sint reme-
dium anime mee. Pater noster. Aue maria.

Dn̄e ihū xp̄e adoro te in sepulchro positū
mirra et aromatibꝯ conditū. depꝛecoꝛ te
ut tua mors sit vita mea. Pater nr̄. Aue maria.

Dn̄e ihū xp̄e adoro te descendentē ad infe-
ros. liberantemꝯ captiuos. depꝛecoꝛ te.
ne pmittas me illuc introire. Pꝛ nꝛ. Aue maria

Dn̄e ihū xp̄e adoro te resurgentē a mortu-
is. ascendentem in celis. sedentemꝯ ad
dexterā patris. depꝛecoꝛ te. miserere mei. nꝛ. Aue.

Dn̄e ihū xp̄e pastor bone. iustos cōserua
peccatores iustifica. omnibꝯ fidelibꝯ miserere. et ꝓpicius esto michi peccatoꝛi. Pꝛ nꝛ. Aue mā

Dn̄e ihū xp̄e fili dei viui. rogo te per illā
amaritudinē quā sustinuisti in cruce max-
ime in illa hora quando aı̄a tua sāctissima de tuo
benedicto corpoꝛe egressa est. miserere aı̄e mee in egres-
su suo. Pꝛ nꝛ. Aue. Collecta ct deuotione addit

ñe ihū xp̄e fili dei viui. qui sāctissime passioıs
tue misteriū bꝛo gregorio famulo tuo mi-
rabiliter reuelasti. da michi misero peccatoꝛi illam
ꝓferre consequi remissionē peccatoꝛ et indulgentiā
quā idem venerabilis antistes tuus et alij sumi
pontifices de plenitudine potestatis aplice oı̄bus
fidelibꝯ vere penitentibꝯ et arma tue passionis de-
uote venerantibꝯ contulerūt. Qui cū deo pꝛe et spū
scō viuis et regnas in scła sclōꝛ. Amen.

misericordissime ihū. O pı̄ssime ihū.
O benignissime ihū. rogo te per tuum
gloriosissimū nomen qꝫ est sup omne
nomen. da michi veram contricionem mee confes

Such a scroll seems designed for private and repeated use. Its decoration would make it a handsome object to hang on a wall, and the script is large enough to read at a distance. The red thread and pinhole at the top of the scroll suggest that it might have been hung to facilitate reading.

☩

Scrolls for private use are mostly designed to be portable. They may be as simple as a shopping list—which usually one does not keep—or as elaborate as some of the splendid decorated prayer scrolls; either way, they are private. "Write whatever you want to remember upon a scroll," says an English rule for women anchorites, religious women who plan to shut themselves away from the world, often by being permanently immured in a cell. Presumably, you will keep the scroll with you at all times.

FIG. 5.7

(*Opposite*) A fifteenth-century Indulgence Roll consisting of seven little prayers (*Septem oraciunculae*) to be said, with Hail Mary and Our Father, in order to gain an indulgence. The prayers begin with "O," and the letters make an attractive chain of alternating blue and red. Decoration at the top and left margins, including a peacock and a dog in fancy dress with a conical collar, resembles the decoration that might be used on the left-hand page of a codex.

Red thread at the top and sides might have been designed for strengthening the scroll when it is hung on a wall. The instructions in red at the top read, "Whoever shall read with a contrite heart these seven little prayers, with as many Hail Marys and Our Fathers, will earn forty-eight thousand and forty years and forty-eight days of indulgence." Harvard University, Houghton Library, MS Typ 286.

Σὺ ὁ Θ̅Σ̅ ἡμῶν ὁ τὸν οὐράνιον
ἄρτον· τὴν τροφὴν τοῦ πα-
τὸς κόσμου· τὸν Κ̅Ν̅ ἡμῶν Ι̅Ν̅
Χ̅Ν̅ ἐξαποστείλας σω-
τῆρα καὶ λυτρω-
τὴν καὶ εὐεργέτην εὐλο-
γοῦντα καὶ ἁγιάζοντα ἡ-
μᾶς, αὐτὸς εὐλόγησον τὴν προ-
θεσιν ταύτην, καὶ πρόσδεξαι
αὐτὴν εἰς τὸ ὑπερουράνιόν σου
θυσιαστήριον· μνημόνευσον
ὡς ἀγαθὸς καὶ φιλάνθρωπος
τῶν προσενεγκάντων καὶ δι' οὓς
προσήγαγον· καὶ ἡμᾶς ἀκατα-
κρίτους διαφύλαξον, ἐν
τῇ ἱερουργίᾳ τῶν θείων σου
μυστηρίων· Ὅτι ἡγίασται καὶ δεδό-
ξασται τὸ πάντιμον καὶ μεγαλοπρεπές
ὄνομα· εὐλόγησον δέσποτα· Ὁ ἱερεὺς· Εὐλο-
γημένη ἡ βασιλεία τοῦ π̅ρ̅Σ̅ καὶ τοῦ
υἱοῦ καὶ τοῦ ἁγίου π̅ν̅Σ̅ νῦν καὶ ἀεί·
Ὁ διάκονος· Ἐν εἰρήνῃ τοῦ Κ̅Υ̅ δεηθῶμεν· Ὑπὲρ τῆς ἄ-
νωθεν εἰρήνης καὶ τῆς σωτηρίας τῶν ψυχῶν ἡμῶν·
Ὑπὲρ τῆς εἰρήνης τοῦ σύμπαντος κόσμου
εὐσταθείας· Ὑπὲρ τοῦ ἁγίου οἴκου
τούτου καὶ τῶν μετὰ πίστεως εὐλα-
Ὑπὲρ τοῦ ἀρχιεπισκόπου ἡμῶν
τοῦ δεῖνος τιμίου πρεσβυτερίου· Ὑπὲρ τῶν εὐσε-
βεστάτων καὶ θεοφυλάκτων ἡμῶν·
Ὑπὲρ τοῦ συμπολεμῆσαι καὶ ὑποτά-
ξαι ὑπὸ τοὺς πόδας· Ὑπὲρ τῆς ἁγίας
μονῆς ταύτης· πάσης πόλεως καὶ
Ὑπὲρ εὐκρασίας ἀέρων εὐφορίας
τῶν καρπῶν τῆς γῆς· Ὑπὲρ πλεόντων
ὁδοιπορούντων νοσούντων·
Ὑπὲρ τοῦ ῥυσθῆναι ἡμᾶς ἀπὸ π̅σ̅
θλίψεως ὀργῆς καὶ ἀνάγκης· Ἀντιλαβοῦ σῶ-
τῆς παναγίας ἀχράντου· τὸ ὑπερευλο-
Ὅτι πρέπει σοι πᾶσα δόξα τιμὴ καὶ

CHAPTER 6

Ritual Scrolls

As an ancient form, a scroll can take on importance from its very construction. It is the way our ancestors did things. We still award academic diplomas, decrees, and citations of various kinds in scroll form as a way to add authority and solemnity to such documents.

Historically, scrolls were used for important documents: they are the traditional way to write the Torah and the Book of Esther, and they are used in the Christian liturgy for solemn moments. In the Byzantine church, scrolls were very frequently used for the liturgy of the eucharist, and hundreds of such scrolls survive (see fig. 6.1). In the Middle Ages important decrees, like those of church councils and law courts were recorded on scrolls. In the Latin West, the *Exultet* scrolls (see pages 160–161) may represent a similar desire to add significance to an important occasion.

FIG. 6.1

(Opposite) A fourteenth-century liturgical scroll of the Byzantine rite, 14 feet long when completely unrolled and 9 inches wide. Written in Greek cursive script on both sides of the scroll, it details the prayers and actions necessary for the celebration of a Byzantine liturgy. The text is titled "The Divine Liturgy of Holy Basil" the first membrane continues with the Great Litany, a series of invocations asking God to bring peace to the world and have mercy on those celebrating the liturgy. The presiding priest would read from the scroll as a presbyter held it open for him with both hands. The red decorative headpiece, now damaged, is the only decoration apart from red initial letters and occasional marginal directions (partway down the right margin is a stylized *ekphone* ("aloud"), meaning that the celebrant is to raise his voice here. Harvard University, Houghton Library MS Typ 416.

Solemn Ceremonies: A Royal Marriage Contract

When the Byzantine princess Theophanu arrived in Rome in 972, she traveled in grand style, with her artists, her architects, and her treasure. She had come to marry Otto, the son of the Holy Roman Emperor Otto the Great. They were married by Pope John XIII, and the next year, when her father-in-law died, she became empress. After her husband Otto II died, in 983, she went on to rule as regent for her young son. A powerful woman in a strange land, Theophanu shocked the court with her fastidious Byzantine ways, insisting on taking a bath every day, and introducing the fork as an implement for transporting food from table to mouth.

A marriage certificate from her husband, listing the extensive dowry given to her on the occasion of her marriage, is a spectacular manuscript on parchment colored with indigo and royal purple, written with gold ink, the sort of preparation reserved for Byzantine imperial decrees. On his wedding day, April 14, 972, the younger Otto set his hand and his ring, with its seal, to this document, as was customary.

The marriage certificate is a scroll made of three membranes, a little over a yard long, framed by decorative gold borders. The gold writing spreads across a surface embellished with circular images of animals and other figures on a purple ground, the spaces between circles decorated with leaves and vines on a blue ground.

Although the charter says that Otto set his hand and seal on the certificate, the seal is missing. Perhaps this is a copy, made for some luxurious, nonlegal purpose. For although the document is in a sense a legal one, its spectacular beauty suggests that it is not a normal one. It lists the extensive gifts from Theophanu's husband, including the lands she received and her rights as empress and as a member of the imperial council. Its elegance reflects the sort of preparation reserved for imperial decrees, such as the letter in the Archivio Segreto Vaticano (Secret Vat-

FIG. 6.2

(*Opposite*) Detail of the Wedding Scroll of the Empress Theophanu. Niedersächsisches Landesarchiv, Wolfenbüttel, 6 Urk Nr. 11.

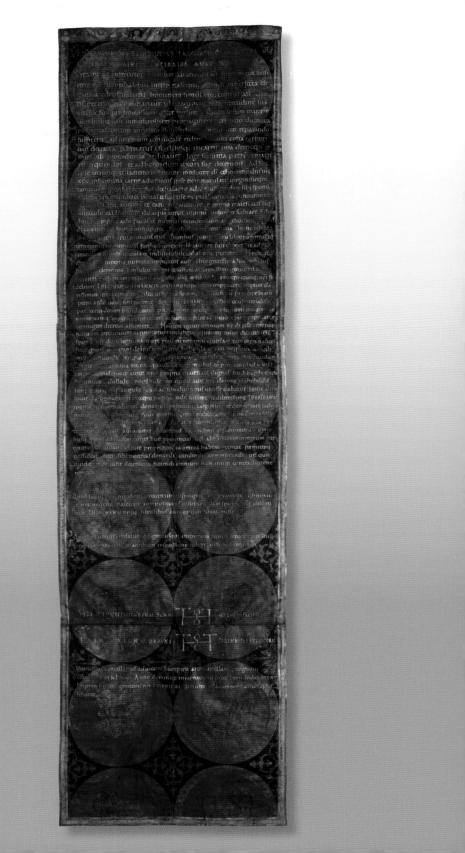

ican archive) written some ten years earlier confirming lands granted by the emperor to the papacy.

Another model may be the magnificent Byzantine letter from Emperor John II Comnenos to Pope Innocent II, also preserved in the Vatican. All three are scrolls, written on purple parchment with gold lettering and decoration, as befits documents of such importance.

Liturgical Scrolls

The medieval liturgy required many texts for the performance of its various ceremonies. These were usually written in codices. Occasionally, however, they took the form of a scroll, for one of two reasons (or sometimes for both). The first was portability—relevant excerpts from large books could be put onto scrolls for processions, for particular ceremonies that took place outside the church, and so on. Second, the importance of the ceremony, or the importance of the person who carried or performed the text, called for the archaic and ceremonial scroll as a suitable vehicle.

✣ PROCESSIONS

In the medieval church, books were an essential part of the furnishing of buildings. Books for reading, for praying, or for singing were created in great numbers for use in the services of the church. Some of these were very beautiful, especially when they had an important function such as bearing the text of the Gospel or the words of the consecration at mass. Books for reading and for singing sometimes grew to be very large, and had to be placed on lecterns or choir stalls to be used by the reader or singer, who turned to the pages needed as the liturgical year progressed.

At special moments in the year, certain ceremonies took place outside the normal area of the church and often involved a procession to and from the ceremony. For example, Palm Sunday begins with the blessing of palms in a location away from the main church and continues with a procession to the church. Candlemas, the commemoration of the Presentation of Jesus in the Temple, involves a procession away from the

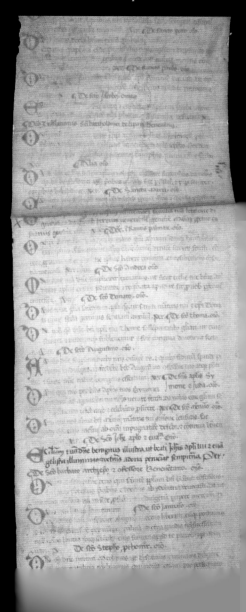

church and back again. The Rogation Days require processions through the city or the surrounding countryside. For these outings, an extract from the big books, containing only the music and words required for the day on a scroll, would be very useful.

The Lorsch Litanies

A scroll that may be tied to a specific moment of political significance is the so-called Lorsch litanies, an eight-foot-long scroll containing a very long litany of the saints—a series of invocations to individual saints by name. Lorsch, near the German city of Worms, was an imperial monastery of great wealth and importance. It was founded in the eighth century with a church rebuilt and dedicated in the presence of Charlemagne. Its library contained a rich treasure of books, including the beautiful golden Gospels of Lorsch, most of them now in the Vatican Library.

The litany on the scroll seems to be connected with Louis the German, Charlemagne's grandson, and his struggle with Charles the Bald—another grandson—for Charlemagne's imperial legacy. It certainly has a level of decoration fit for a king or an emperor.

Extensive litanies like these are normally performed in procession, with the refrain "Pray for us" chanted by all after the name of each saint. The Rogation Days—the Monday, Tuesday, and Wednesday before Ascension Day (which falls on the Thursday that is the fortieth day of Easter)—are an ancient tradition of penitential processions that pass through a city or the countryside, depending on the location of the church or monastery, where the clergy bless crops and fields and the people seek forgiveness for sins.

The Rogation Days in the year 868 fell on May 24–26, during which days there was a synod at Worms at which Louis the German was present. During that meeting, Louis made exchanges of land with Theoderic, the abbot of Lorsch, that considerably enriched the abbey. It may be that Abbot Theoderic presented the scroll to Louis himself during the synod, and that it was used on those days, in Louis' presence, because the litany contains acclamations for Louis and his wife and children, as well as the expected saints. The beautifully decorated scroll calls on the whole army of heaven to protect him. Louis himself, having faced the rebellion of his sons just as he had rebelled against his father, ultimately divided his kingdom among his sons, and at his death was buried at Lorsch.

The back of the scroll contains other interesting materials added later, including prayers, a list of church treasures, and a liturgical play.

The Ambrosian Rite of Milan

Similar to the Lorsch litanies, but specific to a different place and a time some four hundred years later, is the only surviving complete processional scroll featuring the special rites of the church of medieval Milan. This liturgy is called the Ambrosian Rite from its supposed authority, Saint Ambrose of Milan.

The only complete scroll of its kind, it was made around 1300 and contains music for use in the three-day processions of the Ambrosian liturgy of the region of Milan. In the Ambrosian rite, the three Rogation Days come not before Ascension but a week later, in the week before Pentecost; and they are called Litanies rather than Rogations (here "litany" refers not to the list of invocations said in procession, but to the entire complex of ceremonies that occupies each of three days).

The litanies consisted of a series of processions that involved all the clergy in the city of Milan. Starting from the cathedral, a long procession followed a different route on each day, visiting some thirty-two churches of the city over three days. Each day's procession concluded with the celebration of mass at one of the city's principal churches: the first day at St. Ambrose, the second at St. Nazarius, and the final day at St. Lawrence.

During the procession from church to church, a series of pieces called *antiphons* were sung by all in the procession. The antiphons reflect a penitential mood: the first antiphon says "Repent and return to me with your whole heart, says the Lord, in fasting, weeping, and lamenting; for I do not desire the death of a sinner, but that he should turn back, and live."

On arrival at the various churches, first a prayer is said, then a solo piece called a *responsory* is sung by one of the clergy; both of these refer

FIG. 6.4
The Lorsch litany scroll, made in the 860s by the monks of the imperial abbey of Lorsch, near Worms, possibly for presentation to Charlemagne's grandson Louis the German during the synod of Worms in 868. Decorated with colored inks and a beautiful border, it is 8 feet long, and contains the names of 524 saints, each of whom is asked to pray for us. At the top the litany begins "IN CHRISTI NOMINE INCIPIT LAETANIA" in red, and then reads across each line:

Kyrie eleison
Christe eleison
Kyrie eleison

Christe audi nos
Christe audi nos
Christe audi nos

And then come the saints: "Sancta Maria" three times; then three archangels, Michael, Gabriel, and Raphael; the disciples, John, Peter, Paul, etc.; then the long list of saints, which continues for another 7 feet. Frankfurt am Main, Universitätsbibliothek Johann Christian Senckenberg, MS Barth. 179.

to the saint to whom the church is dedicated. The procession then moves on to the next church. A map of the three initeraries would show that the procession visited each of the major churches, inside and outside the walls of Milan, on one of the three days, always beginning and ending at the cathedral.

This particular scroll seems to be a document for someone who leads the singers. It's not a fancy scroll, but instead quite small, rolled on a stick, and protected with a leather cover. It includes not only the antiphons sung by the full choir, but also the solo responsories, which are labeled in the margins "L" (Lector), "Not" (Notarius), "Subd" (Subdiaconus), to indicate that the scroll might be handed in turn to the those who were to sing the responsories (or it might have remained in the possession of the functionary whose duty was to see to it that the music was sung in the proper order and in the correct way). One can imagine this scroll, and perhaps others like it, carried reverently on these long ceremonial trips around medieval Milan.

Another scroll (called *rotulus letaniarum*) contained the prayers said in each church, and others just the antiphons and other materials sung by the choir (an incomplete one of these latter survives in Milan).

The complexities of the liturgy of the medieval cathedral of Milan is

FIG. 6.5

A musical scroll for the three days of processions in medieval Milan knows as Litanies; in the Ambrosian rite of the city, the clergy went from the cathedral to a series of churches—a different itinerary each day—and sang as they went. This scroll contains the music for the processions.

The scroll was written, as is typical, on one side only, beginning with what would be the outside end; evidently the full length of the scroll was assembled and glued before writing began, since the scroll is not long enough to hold the complete music for these ceremonies, and the scribe turned the roll over and wrote the remaining text and music on the back. New Haven, Beinecke Rare Book and Manuscrpt Library, MS Beinecke 810.

matched by the grand hierarchy of its clergy, totaling more than ninety clerics of assorted rank including:

The archbishop
Seven cardinal priests, lead by the archpriest with his staff
Seven cardinal deacons, lead by the archdeacon with his staff
The subdeacons, led by their *primicerius* (the first in rank)
The leader of the priests
The notaries, with their *primicerius*
Sixteen lectors, with their *primicerius* and master
    the second lector is called *secundicerius*
    the next 4 in are called *clavicularii* (keepers of the keys)
    the last 11 are called *terminarii*
Four *magistri scolarum* (masters of the choir)
Sixteen *custodes* (custodians of the treasury), under their *cimilarcha*
    (master of the ashes)
    8 senior, divided into 4 *cicendelarii* (candle-lighters) and 4
        ostiarii (doorkeepers)
    8 junior
Twenty *vetuli* (or *veglioni*, those who keep watch), 10 male
    and 10 female
the staff-bearer of the secular authority, or of the Viscount

Excerpts from the directions for the litany ceremonies provide a vivid picture of the complex hierarchy of the cathedral and of the importance of this highly urban ritual. The ceremony begins with the blessing and the imposition of ashes, a sign of penitence (as in the Roman church on Ash Wednesday). Each section of the procession is led by a cross: one for the subdeacons, one for the notaries, one for the priests (with their primicerius), and the viscount:

And in these three days the assigned priest and the chief doorkeeper take turns carrying the golden cross before the cardinal priests and deacons, and one of them should always dine with the archbishop, but on the third day, both of them. [Clearly the days are penitential: they have put ashes on their heads, but there is dinner at the end!]

And the two persons who are behind them who carry the ashes, should carry one cross before the subdeacons, and another before the notaries, and should dine with them. And the two lesser ebdomadarii [officials for the week] likewise should carry a cross before the primicerius of the priests, one of whom on the third day will dine with them, and will give twelve denarii. Likewise two lesser doorkeepers shall take turns carrying a cross before the viscount, and one of them on the third day shall dine with him.

At each of the various churches they visit, there is a reading, and a chant (responsory), which is sung from the music scroll. Note the scroll containing prayers that is placed on the altar in each church by the archbishop's scroll bearer:

And be it known, that the secundicerius [of the lectors] reads the first lection, and the notarius sings the responsory; then the notarius reads the second lection, and the lector the responsory. And thus they continue to take turns reading and singing until the last [lection], except the four lections of the primicerius of the lectors, namely at St. Victor ad corpus, and at St. Stephen, and at St. Eustorgius, and at St. George. And the deacons likewise take turns reading the gospels. And the rotularius [scroll-bearer] of the archbishop always carries the scroll, and ministers to the archbishop; but if the archbishop is absent, he who carries the golden cross carries the same scroll, and places it on the various altars, from which the priest takes it and says the prayers.

These ceremonies were important for the well-being of the city of Milan, and it was therefore important that they be carried out correctly. The processional scrolls that contain the music are perhaps made in that form mostly for portability (but then one wonders why all three day's worth of music is put on a single scroll, rather than having a scroll for each day).

✛ THE BENEVENTO SCROLLS

A group of beautifully executed liturgical scrolls is connected with the cathedral of Benevento, a prominent city in the early Middle Ages. The city was the capital of a Lombard duchy—later principality—in southern Italy, and a cultural and political center that faded in the wake of Carolingian invasions. The area ruled from Benevento developed a characteristic writing style called Beneventan script, which was later perfected at the nearby monastery of Montecassino. A series of illustrated scrolls was designed for use by the Archbishop of Benevento: the idea of scrolls like these spread through southern Italy, producing a group of the most interesting scrolls made in the Middle Ages.

What is fascinating about the Beneventan scrolls is that they are intended to be sung, and unrolled while they are sung. As they are unrolled, large illustrations, sometimes painted upside down, from the singer's point of view, appear right side up to anybody who is near the pulpit where the singing takes place, providing a sort of multimedia event of sound, text, and image.

Benevento, previously the undisputed center of power in southern Italy, had been reduced—by Arab invasion, Byzantine domination, and local squabbling among competing princes—to a secondary role. However, as political power waned, the church filled the vacuum. The bishops of Benevento came to have increasing influence, and the cathedral gained prominence. Meanwhile, the relics of the apostle Saint Bartholomew, brought to Benevento in 838 and preserved in a basilica adjoining the cathedral, attracted pilgrims, and the political void was easily filled by the authority of the bishop.

In 969, Bishop Landolf, also a nobleman of the Lombard nation, became Benevento's first archbishop when the diocese was raised to an archdiocese by Pope John XIII. This event had its political usefulness: it strengthened the church against Byzantine incursions in the south. Archbishop Landolf's elevation and reign were marked, among other things, by a series of splendid scrolls designed to celebrate his new dignity.

The Pontifical Scroll

What is probably the earliest surviving scroll of Benevento is associated with Landolf very clearly, since at the end of it, in big gold letters, it states, "I BELONG TO LANDOLF THE BISHOP" (*Landolfi episcopi sum*). There's no doubt whose scroll this is, and it is clearly one for a bishop to use in performing ceremonies that only a bishop performs: consecrating churches, ordaining clergy, and so on. Such a series of ceremonies is often written in a book called a pontifical, and the bishop can carry it with him as he travels through his diocese.

FIG. 6.6

The pontifical scroll of Landolf I, Archbishop of Benevento (tenth century), made of five membranes originally held together by parchment strips woven through slits in the parchment sheets. The scroll is 11½ feet long. The ordination of priests is illustrated here. Candidates arrive from the bishop's left. The bishop, in the center, places his hand on the heads of a group of priests who are already wearing priestly stoles. The archbishop, with a square gold nimbus, holds the end of his golden archiepiscopal pallium between his fingers. The directions conclude "And while they are prostrate on the ground the following preface is said by the bishop in the tone of readings." The prayer itself, beginning "Sit nobis fratres communis oratio," is written below the picture. Rome, Biblioteca Casanatense, MS 724 (II).

Landolf's pontifical is a beautifully illustrated scroll that shows how to carry out each of various ceremonies by picturing the ceremony itself. In addition to the words the bishop should pronounce, the scroll includes directions for the ordinations of various ranks of clergy, in ascending order: doorkeepers, lectors, exorcists, acolytes, subdeacons, deacons, and priests.

The illustrations focus on the bishop. Depicted with a large square halo above his head (a square nimbus designates living persons), his figure is larger than everybody else's. In several pictures he wears the gold pallium around his shoulders, a symbol of his status as archbishop. The pictures follow the texts that they illustrate, giving a careful rendition of the instructions.

The bishop always faces to the right and is larger than the other figures, who are situated at a respectful distance. On his right he is accompanied by priests wearing golden stoles. Those to be ordained arrive from his left.

The Benedictional Scroll

Another beautiful scroll, probably also made for Landolf (he is named in a poem near the end of the roll), was designed to be used on the vigil of Easter for the ceremonies involving baptism: the blessing of baptismal water and the baptism of new Christians. It reads, in capital letters at its beginning, "BENEDICTIO FONTIS" (blessing of the font). Like the pontifical scroll, this one was held open to the portion the bishop needed at each moment of the ceremony by an assistant so the bishop could perform the various functions that required his hands to be free. And like the other scroll, it is filled with glorious illustrations of the ceremonies as they unfold. They are not by the same artist, but they are in the same style; the bishop with his square halo is painted on bare parchment without frame or background.

A chief feature of this scroll is the very long prayer the bishop says as he consecrates the water of baptism. Many illustrations are threaded

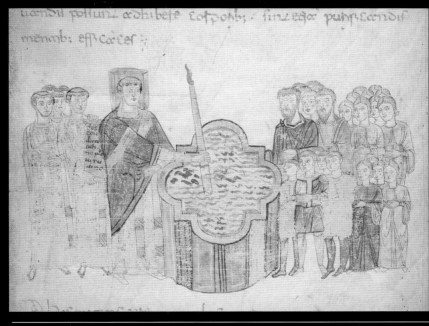

FIG. 6.7

The benedictional scroll of Landolf I, about 11 inches wide and 16 feet long, contains the text recited by the bishop when he blesses the water to be used in baptism during the long ceremonies of the vigil of Easter. In this picture the bishop immerses the candle in the font (*"Hic mittis cereum in fonte"* [Here you put the candle into the font]: note that the instructions, in red below the picture, are addressed directly to the bishop).

The bishop with his own hands lowers the lit candle into the baptismal water. A deacon wearing a stole stands behind the bishop and holds the liturgical scroll—this very scroll!—on which is transcribed the passage the bishop is saying: *"Descendat in hanc plenitudinem."* In an earlier picture the bishop himself holds the scroll, reciting the introductory prayer; here, in order to lower the candle into the baptismal water, he has handed the scroll to a deacon. To the right of the font are arranged children and parents, divided into male and female. Rome, Biblioteca Casanatense, MS 724 (II).

throughout the text showing the bishop performing various acts: inserting a burning candle into the water; the creation of water and the division of water from land at creation; two miracles of Moses associated with water; the baptism of Jesus; and the wedding at Cana, when water was changed into wine. The lavish decorations are a celebration of the grandeur and solemnity of the office of Archbishop of Benevento, to be admired on occasions when the bishop could display his roll at leisure.

Exultet: *Pictures and Music*

Landolf possessed a third magnificent scroll, also for use on the vigil of Easter, containing the words and the music for the blessing of the paschal candle. In the liturgy of Benevento this blessing takes place not at the beginning of the ceremonies, as in the Roman rite, but after a series of readings. The archbishop does not use the scroll personally: he assigns a deacon to sing the blessing, and hands him the scroll with words, music, and pictures much like the pontifical and benedictional scrolls. The first picture on the scroll, in fact, is a picture of the archbishop handing the scroll to the deacon who is to sing.

It begins with the words of the blessing, "Exultet iam angelica turba celorum" (Let the angelic choir of heaven rejoice) and continues with a celebration of the transition from night to day, from winter to spring, from death to new life in baptism. The text is filled with poetic imagery recalling the passage of the children of Israel through the Red Sea, the pillar of fire that illuminated the night, the work of the bees who made the wax of the candle, and the flame itself; this was all symbolized by the candle that is to be blessed, whose flame will spread throughout the church and the city. Sung in the darkened cathedral with the light of a single candle, the effect must have been deeply mysterious and affecting.

This scroll, like Landolf's other scrolls, is magnificently illustrated, embellished with glints of gold that can be seen from a distance, especially when the deacon goes up into the pulpit to sing.

The bad news is that Landolf's scroll is lost. We can be certain that it existed, because a copy was made in the later tenth century for the use of the nearby convent of Saint Peter's Outside the Walls in Benevento. On the copy, an extraordinary object, although it is now fragmentary, an illustration at the end shows a certain Iohannes presenting the scroll to Saint Peter, and in the text of the scroll, the concluding invocations include prayers for the abbess of St. Peter's and her congregation.

Despite the alterations, we can be sure that the St. Peter's scroll is a copy of one originally made for Archbishop Landolf in or after 969, because it matches in many ways the other two liturgical rolls made for him, and, in particular, because of the extraordinary attention given to the archbishop in the illustrations. In the copy, the part of the text that differs from Landolf's original comes after the scene of Iohannes and St. Peter; this suggests that a different final presentation scene, on the model of "LANDOLFI EPISCOPI SUM" in the pontifical scroll, may have been present in Landolf's original.

The idea of using a scroll for the text and the music of the *Exultet* was not unique to Benevento, but it may well have started there, with Landolf's scroll. Wherever it started, the idea caught on fast, and in southern Italy many churches, most of them cathedrals (that is, churches with bishops), created long illustrated scrolls for the special ceremony of the *Exultet*. Some twenty-five such scrolls survive, all but one of them from southern Italy.

At some point somebody had the absolutely brilliant idea of turning the pictures—not only of the *Exultet* but other events and people referred to in the text like the Red Sea, the Pillar of Fire, the bees—upside down so they are right side up when they appear over the top of the pulpit as the deacon sings about them, and the whole thing becomes a sort of cinematic display. Many though not all of the surviving *Exultet* scrolls have their pictures this way, apparently designed for viewing during the ceremony. This was not the original idea, to judge from Landolf's scroll, which was illustrated like his other two scrolls. But the idea of reversing the pictures (which probably originated somewhere else—perhaps

The opening image of the tenth-century *Exultet* scroll of St. Peter's convent, Benevento, a copy of a scroll made for Archbishop Landolf I. Here the archbishop, magnificently enthroned in a golden arch and wearing the archbishop's pallium around his shoulders, hands the scroll—the very scroll we're looking at—to a deacon (with his stole over the left shoulder), who will use the scroll to sing the blessing of the Paschal candle, beginning "Exultet iam angelica turba celorum." Vatican City, Biblioteca Apostolica Vaticana, MS Lat. 9820.

The opening image of the twelfth-century *Exultet* roll at Benevento, modeled like the *Exultet* of St. Peter's (fig. 6.9A) on the lost Landolf scroll, but not so elegant. Here again the bishop plays a primary role, handing the scroll to the deacon for use during the *Exultet*. When it came to the library in Rome this scroll was attached to the two beautiful tenth-century Landolf scrolls (figs. 6.6 and 6.7, pages 155 and 157); perhaps this scroll was made as a substitute for the earlier one now lost. This scroll is modernized—it has the Roman text rather than the Beneventan, and the pictures are inverted. Rome, Biblioteca Casanatense MS 724 (III).

FIG. 6.9A

A section from the tenth-century *Exultet* scroll of St Peter's, Benevento, modeled on the scroll of Archbishop Landolf. Here the bishop lights the candle while the deacon sings; the deacon's text is visible on the scroll: "Ut superne benedictionis munus accomodes," a passage from the Beneventan text of the *Exultet*. This text, however, appears nowhere on the scroll as it is currently constituted because the original scroll has been erased, reversed, and rewritten with the Roman text, which does not contain those words. In the text panels the original gold initial letters, text, and notation, oriented in the same direction as the picture, are barely visible under the more recent, reversed writing. Vatican City, Biblioteca Apostolica Vaticana, MS Lat. 9820.

FIG. 6.9B

A similar image from the twelfth-century *Exultet* of Benevento. The scene takes place inside a church building; the deacon, holding the scroll, is in an ornate pulpit, with an eagle and various other decorations. The candle is lit by the bishop. Rome, Biblioteca Casanatense MS 724 (III).

at Bari, where an early-eleventh-century scroll is the oldest one with reversed pictures) was taken up, even at Benevento.

A twelfth-century *Exultet* scroll from Benevento is based on the pictures in the Landolf scroll but has its pictures reversed. It was at one time attached to the two surviving Landolf scrolls, and perhaps was made as a substitute for Landolf's original *Exultet*.

Even the beautiful tenth-century scroll of St. Peter's was subjected to this new idea. In the twelfth century, it was completely revamped. The scroll was taken apart, its original text almost entirely erased, and a new text, with its music, was written in the opposite direction so that the pictures would now be upside down with respect to the words. The result was not perfect, since the new words were the text of the Roman liturgy, not the Beneventan text that had originally been there; as a result, the pictures don't always correspond to passages in the new text. It must have seemed important to preserve these beautiful pictures, and to have an up-to-date scroll with Roman text and reversed pictures, because the beautiful original was mutilated to produce its "upgraded" version. We can still see the erased original text, with its handsome gold letters, here and there, under the now-reversed Roman text.

Only in southern Italy, in the area that practiced the regional Beneventan liturgy, were elaborately illustrated *Exultet* scrolls used. At its origin, the Beneventan *Exultet*—with its text and music taken from the Beneventan liturgy—characterized the regional liturgy. However, the practice of using a scroll for the *Exultet* survived the change from the Beneventan text to the Roman. Most of the twenty-five *Exultet* rolls from southern Italy feature the newer text from the Roman rite.

These various versions of the *Exultet* text were written on scrolls in order to lend importance, solemnity, and magnificence to the occasion. The phenomenon may have originated with Landolf himself, since, as noted, what may be the original *Exultet* scroll was a companion to two others made for him. Even though Landolf's scroll was not used by the archbishop himself—the *Exultet* is always sung by a deacon—it is clearly his. The scroll pictures the bishop enthroned, looking like a Byzantine emperor or perhaps a deity. The very first picture in the scroll, its headpiece, shows the bishop handing the scroll to the deacon. He is lending it to his appointed assistant, offering an object of ceremonial episcopal splendor.

FIG. 6.10

The second *Exultet* scroll of Montecassino, here opened for inspection. Montecassino, Biblioteca dell'Abbazia Exultet 2. Photo Giulio Menna.

POSTLUDE

Roll It Back Up

The patrons and scribes of the Middle Ages knew what they were doing when they made scrolls. They are the same people who ordered, made, and used books in codex form. But when they made a scroll, as we have seen, they had their reasons for doing so. They did not make many scrolls, as we know if we compare the number of books that survive to the number of scrolls. At the university where I teach, a repository of rare books and manuscripts, called the Houghton Library, owns about five thousand medieval manuscripts from western Europe in codex form, but just eleven scrolls. Perhaps that ratio is about the same as it was in the Middle Ages. As we have learned, many scrolls were made to be temporary—roles for actors, cheat sheets for poets, and other scrolls for immediate use—but overall fewer scrolls were created in the period of the codex.

This book has proposed four basic reasons someone might choose the scroll format, and its central chapters are oriented to those reasons. We have seen that, even though every scroll corresponds to one of those reasons, many of them may represent more than one motivation, and that there is a sort of unity of concept about the scroll that goes beyond any single practical reason. A scroll is a representation of continuity, something potentially

---

FIG. 7.1
(*Opposite*) A steel-rolling mill. Rosenfeld Images, LTD. / Science Source.

without an end. The act of writing, similarly, produces a single long line, even though the line must be broken into pieces by the physical limitations of margins. It is like creating an endless thread.

Many scrolls, now as then, exist because of this desire for continuity. Sometimes the continuity is real and necessary, and sometimes it's symbolic. Magnetic recording tape, cinema film, and other media require an unbroken continuity in order to work.

Sometimes that continuity must be broken because of the nature of the medium. Cinema is, after all, made of a series of separate images; the credits scrolling by at the end of a movie are made up of individual lines of text. Comic books and graphic novels simulate continuous time, and are drawn in strips that we are to imagine form a continuous series. The texts on our computer screens, even when they are made of individual lines, create a flowing continuous scrolling column. Punched rolls for player pianos and punched tape for earlier transcription machines (wire services) and computers needed a continuous surface on which information could be recorded, and read back in a regulated timing as the scroll passes by. Seismographs and certain kinds of devices for recording weather (temperature, barometric pressure) were once designed to trace a line onto a continuous paper grid representing the passage of time.

Scrolls are used, now as then, when it is important not to fold or otherwise mutilate the material itself. The materials must be maintained intact for now—for storage or for transport—even though the scroll may ultimately be separated into pieces. Sometimes it is not known how long the pieces will be, as with bolts of fabric; other times, the pieces are predetermined, as with paper towels, where the scroll gets shorter with use. In a way, this is the opposite of medieval mortuary rolls, which grow longer as they travel.

All these uses of scrolls as we have them today are essentially practical. The reasons for making scrolls in the Middle Ages was also largely practical, *except* for the archaizing instinct, which led to the production of such beautiful objects as Theophanu's wedding scroll and the illustrated *Exultet*s. Still, in some cultures today, scrolls maintain their important place: in Japanese and Chinese art, in Jewish religious practices, and, for those who can remember the film "Planet of the Apes" (1968), in the sacred scrolls that govern the culture of that planet. And at the end of the neck of every violin, viola, and cello, and at the top of every Ionic column, is a reminder of the timelessness of this format.

As I compose this text on my computer, I realize that above the line that I type now is a very long column of text. If that text were to be printed without any of the tiresome page breaks to which you, reader, have been subjected, it would be on a very long column of paper. The only suitable way to store it would be to roll it up. That way, it would be a successor to the beautiful illustrated scrolls of the Middle Ages.

Acknowledgments

A seminar at Harvard University on medieval scrolls taught me a great deal, and helped organize the database and bibliography that can be found at medievalscrolls.com. My fellow teachers were Beverly Kienzle, William Stoneman, and Timothy Baker. The staffs of the Houghton Library and the Harvard Law School Library (in particular Karen Beck), were enormously generous in allowing us to view scrolls at close hand, and in helping with the exhibition of scrolls that we undertook in connection with the seminar. The members of the seminar, to whom I owe a great deal, were: Yashua Bhattil, Marina Connelly, Helen Cushman, Rebecca Frankel, Leland Grigoli, Patrick McCoy; Sean McLaughlin, Emerson Morgan, Arlene Navarro, Scott Possiel, Nicole Pulichene, Zoey Walls, Porter White, Honor Wilkinson, Katherine Wrisley Shelby.

The medievalscrolls.com website was supported by grants from the Lasky-Barajas Fund, with the encouragement, assistance, and support of Judson Harward. Technical aspects were excuted by Jeff Emanuel, James Hudson, and their team. Scott Possiel, Emily Izer, and Lane Baker have contributed substantially to the completeness and the accuracy of the website. An associated online module about scrolls is available from HarvardX in their course on the History of the Book.

Many scholars have contributed suggestions, references, and expertise to the information in this book. A few whose specific contributions have allowed me to present an expertise far from my own are: Steen Clemmensen, Farum, Denmark, along with colleagues whom he consulted, for a comprehensive analysis of surviving armorial materials, assisting substantially in determining which are actually in roll form; Lisa Fagin Davis, for help with chronicle rolls; Jeffrey Hamburger, for his eagle eye in spotting and signaling medieval scrolls; Geof Huth, for help with New York Supreme Court of Adjudicature legal rolls; Melissa McCormick, for expertise on Asian scrolls; Kay Kaufman Shelemy, for expertise on Ethiopian scrolls; Nino Zchomelidze, for information on the Theophanu roll and related documents.

The authorities of many libraries and other institutions have generously given their time and expertise to answer questions, provide access, and permit the reproduction of the materials in their care. These are acknowledged at suitable places, and together they form a community of knowledge and of inquiry that is one of the glories of our culture.

The Rothenberg Research Fund at Harvard provided a generous subvention that allowed for the handsome color images in this book.

Maribeth Payne of W. W. Norton was the first reader of this book, and her suggestions for improving it have made if far better that it might have been. Quynh Do has seen it through its maturing process, helping with substantial editing, suggestions, and encouragement. To them, along with Grant Phelps, Nancy Green, and others at W. W. Norton, my sincere gratitude.

Notes

Chapter 1: Introduction to Scrolls

8   Saint Jerome, the fourth-century translator: For Saint Jerome's technical terms, see Evaristo Arns, *La technique du livre d'après Saint Jérôme* (Paris: E. de Boccard, 1953), pp. 118–21.

20   Pliny the Elder: Text from Frederic G. Kenyon (trans.), *Books and Readers in Ancient Greece and Rome* (Oxford: Clarendon, 1932), pp. 122–24.

25   the elder Pliny left 160 volumes: Kenyon, *Books and Readers*, p. 60.

25   the Byzantine historian Zonaras: Teodor Büttner-Wobst, *Ioannes Zonarae Epitomae historiarum.* 3 vols. *Corpus scriptorum historiae byzantinae* (Bonn: Weber, 1891–97), vol. 3, p. 131.

25   "It cannot be denied": Kenyon, *Books and Readers*, p. 67.

27   Verginius Rufus: Pliny the Younger, *Letters*, Book 2, letter 1, in Colin Wells, *The Roman Empire* (Cambridge, MA: Harvard University Press, 1992), pp. 153–54.

31   Dr. W. Brent Seales: "Technology Unlocks Secrets of a Biblical Scroll," *New York Times*, Sept. 22, 2016, p. A9; "From Damage to Discovery via Virtual Unwrapping, https://www.youtube.com/watch?v=D9IXX-VJJzA&feature=youtu.be.

31   Dr. Vito Mocella: Vito Mocella, "The Quest of Lost Ancient Literature: The Secrets of Herculaneum Papyri Revealed Through Synchrotron Based Techniques, " lecture in the Cultural and Textual Exchanges series, University of Iowa, January 20, 2017, http://eurasianmss.lib.uiowa.edu/lectures/#Vito-Mocella-Lecture.

32   The codex format arrived with Christianity: See Colin Henderson Rob-

erts, "The Codex," *Proceedings of the British Academy* 40 (1954): 169–204 and plate, unnumbered page; Roberts and T. C. Skeat, *The Birth of the Codex* (London: Oxford University Press, 1987).

32   Pope Gregory the Great: *Gregorii magni Papae Registrum epistolarum* 5.53a, ed. Paulus Ewald and Ludovicus M. Hartmann, *Monumenta Germaniae Historica Epistolae*, 2 vols. (Berlin: Weidmann, 1957), vol. 2, p. 355.

33   Guillaume Durandus: Gulielmus Durandus, *Rationale divinorum officiorum*, ed. A. Davril and T. M. Thibodeau, in Victor M. Schmidt (trans.),"Some Notes on Scrolls in the Middle Ages," *Quaerendo* 41 (2011): 373–83 at p. 381.

Chapter 2: Scrolls That Grow

41   New York State has a series: I am grateful to Geof Huth, Chief Records Officer / Chief Law Librarian of the Unified Court System of New York, for providing information on these scrolls.

44   the Fine Roll for 1263–64: Information from Huw Ridgeway, "The exploits of two Dorset Knights at the Battle of Lewes and on the Fine Roll," January 2012, online at http://www.finerollshenry3.org.uk/content/month/fine_of_the_month.html for people, places, and subjects mentioned in the Fine Rolls.

49   An excerpt from the list of 1588–89: From New Year's gift roll: http://www.larsdatter.com/gifts/New Year's Gifts for Queen Elizabeth, from *The Progress and Public Processions of Queen Elizabeth*.

53   Jean II de Marigny: Jean Dufour, *Recueil des rouleaux des morts (VIIIe siècle-vers 1536)*, publié sous la direction de Jean Favier. Recueil des historiens de la France. Obituaires. Série in-4o ; t. 8. 5 vols. (Paris: Diffusion de Boccard, 2005–2013), vol. 3, p. 102, no. 300.

56   "assent and avysement": Samuel Pegge, ed., *The Forme of Cury; a roll of ancient English cookery, compiled, about A.D. 1390, by the master-cooks of King Richard II, presented afterwards to Queen Elizabeth, by Edward, lord Stafford, and now in the possession of Gustavus Brander, esq.* (London: J. Nichols, 1780), p. xvi; "common pottages,", p. 2; "Cranys and Herons," p. 92; "Mawmenny," p. 88.

57   what King Richard II enjoyed: From London, British Library Harleian

MS 4016, edited as one of *Two Fifteenth-Century Cookery-Books*, ed. Thomas Austin (London: Early English Text Society, 1888), pp. 67–69.

59   mixture of pharmacy, medicine, and the practice of incantations: Bern, Burgerbibl., Cod. 803.

59   "+ [make the sign of the cross]:" Walter Henzen, "Der Rotulus von Mülinen. Codex 803 der Burgerbibliothek Bern," in *Geschichte, Deutung, Kritik. Literaturwissenschafliche Beiträge dargebracht zum 65. Geburtstag Werner Kohlschmidts*, ed. Mari Bindschedler and Paul Zinsli (Bern: Francke, 1969), pp. 13–27 at p. 15.

62   "In every affection": *De arte physicali*, ed. D'Arcy Power (New York: William Wood, 1922), p. xxiv.

62   Several surviving medieval scrolls: Two such scrolls of the fourteenth century are now in Kassel (Murhardsches Bibliothek MSS 8o Med. 11.1 and 11.2).

66   "When busie at my Book": Originally published in Eirenaeus Philalethes, *Ripley Reviv'd: or, an Exposition upon Sir George Ripley's Hermetico-Poetical Works. Containing the plainest and most excellent Discoveries of the most hidden Secrets of the Ancient Philosophers, that were ever yet published. Written by Eirenaeus Philalethes an Englishman, stiling himself Citizen of the World.* (London: Printed by Tho. Ratcliff and Nat. Thompson, for William Cooper at the Pelican in Little-Britain, 1678).

Chapter 3: Representing Space and Time: The Long Red Line

86   the forty-two encampments: See Andrea Worm, "'Ista est Jerusalem.' Intertextuality and Visual Exegesis in Peter of Poitiers' *Compendium historiae in genealogia Christi* and Werner Rolevinck's *Fasciculus temporum*," in *Imagining Jerusalem in the Medieval West*, ed. Lucy Donkin and Hanna Vorholt (New York: Oxford University Press, 2012), pp. 123–62, at p. 142.

Chapter 4: Performers' Scrolls

104   "that the composition of the scrolls": Elisabeth Lalou, "Les rolets de théâtre: étude codicologique," in *Théâtre et spectacle hier et aujourd'hui, Moyen âge et Renaissance. Actes du 115e congrès national des sociétés savantes, Avignon, 1990* (Paris: Éditions du CTHS, 1991), pp. 51–71, at

p. 55, citing P.-E. Giraud and Ulysse Chevalier, *Le Mystère des trois Dons joué à Romans en 1509* (Lyon: 1887), p. 482, trans. T. F. Kelly.

106   Poets in medieval pictures: Richard H. Rouse, "Roll and Codex: The Transmission of the Works of Reinmar von Zweter," *Paläographie 1981; Colloquium des Comité international de paléographie. München, 15.–18. September 1981*, ed. Gabriel Silagi. Münchener Beiträge zur Mediävistik und Renaissance-Forschung 32 (Munich: Arbeo-Gesellschaft, 1982), pp. 107–23, plates XI–XV at 115–116; further examples of poetic rolls, pp. 118–20.

107   "When I showed these little verses": *The Early Medieval Sequence* (Berkeley : University of California Press, 1977), p. 1, trans. (altered by T. F. Kelly) by Richard Crocker from the Latin in Wolfram von den Steinen, *Notker der Dichter und seine geistige Welt*, 2 vols. (Bern: Francke, 1978), vol. 2, pp. 8–10.

113   "A lady claims a missal": Cited in Richard Rouse, "Roll and Codex," pp. 120–21, from Helen M. Cam, *The Hundred and the Hundred Rolls* (London: Methuen, 1930), p. 182, and R. M. Wilson, *The Lost Literature of Medieval England*, 2d ed. (London: Methuen, 1970), p. 163.

113   a scroll originally from Picardy: In Lambeth Palace, London Misc. Rolls 1435.

114   Fig 4.6: For details on this image see Christopher Page, "An English motet of the 14th century in performance: two contemporary images," *Early Music* 25 (1997), 7–32.

115   "Unus rotulus de cantu": The lost scrolls of Branscomb and Leominster are cited in Andrew Wathey, "Lost Books of Polyphony in England: A List to 1500," *Royal Musical Association Research Chronicle*, No. 21 (1988): 1–19.

117   The scholar Karl Kügle: "Two Abbots and a Rotulus: New Light on Brussels 19606," in *Quomodo Cantabimus Canticum? Studies in Honor of Edward H. Roesner*, ed. D. B. Cannata, G. Ilnitchi Currie, R. C. Mueller, and J. L. Nádas (Middleton, WI: American Institute of Musicology, 2008), pp. 145–85.

118   a similar scroll survives in Paris: In the Collection de Picardie of the Bibliothèque Nationale de France (coll. Picardie 67, f. 67).

118   John, 2nd Baron Segrave: On the Segrave scroll, see Andrew Wathey, ed. *Berkeley Castle, Select Roll 55: Motets and Sequences from the Early Fourteenth Century* (Newton Abbot, England: Antico Edition, 1991).

Chapter 5: Private Scrolls: Amulets, Charms, and Prayers

126   ABRAXAS and ABRACADABRA: On amuletic formulas, see Don C. Skemer, "Amulet Rolls and Female Devotion in the Late Middle Ages," *Scriptorium* 55 (2001): 197–227 and pl. 51, p.198.

127   One amulet scroll of the fourteenth or early fifteenth century: Now in a private collection, this is described by Skemer, "Amulet Rolls," pp. 202–14; transcription and photo, pp. 224–28.

135   "The daily handling of this roll": *British Museum Quarterly* 4 (1929–30), p. 111, on a fourteenth-century Dutch roll decorated with gold (British Library MS Egerton 3044).

141   "Write whatever you want to remember": Robert W. Ackerman and Roger Dahood, *Ancrene riwle: Introduction and Part I* (Binghamton, NY: Center for Medieval and Early Renaissance Studies, 1984), pp. 74–75.

Chapter 6: Ritual Scrolls

146   Byzantine letter from Emperor John II Comnenos: The letter written ten years earlier is Archivio Segreto Vaticano AA Arm. I-XVIII, 18; the letter from the emperor to Innocent II is Archivio Segreto Vaticano, AA Arm. I-XVIII, 402r.

148   "The Rogation Days in the year 843": On the possible political significance of the Lorsch litany scroll, see Eric Joseph Goldberg, *Struggle for Empire: Kingship and Conflict Under Louis the German, 817–876* (Ithaca, NY: Cornell University Press, 2009), pp. 291–92.

152   directions for the litany ceremonies: Marcus Magistretti, *Beroldus sive ecclesiae ambrosianae mediolanensis kalendarium et ordines saec. XII* (Milan: Josephi Giovanola, 1894), pp. 118–20, the author's translation.

Index

Page numbers in *italics* refer to illustrations.

Thomas Forrest Kelly is professor of music at Harvard University. The author of *Capturing Music* and *Music Then and Now*, he lives in Cambridge, Massachusetts.